When Language Fails

When Language Fails

When Language Fails

Ontological Pluralism and the Limits of Moral Resolution

Bry Willis

Philosophics Press ◐ 2026

First Edition

ISBN (Hardback): 978-1-972025-01-7
ISBN (Paperback): 978-1-972025-00-0

ORCiD: 0009-0005-0016-5694

Published by *Philosophics Press*,
Cambridge, Massachusetts
Printed in the country of distribution
< philosophics.blog >

Library of Congress Catalogue Number: 2026905652

Subject Keywords:
Philosophy of language
Ontology
Epistemology
Moral pluralism
Incommensurability
Hermeneutics

For those whose world is not the one presumed.

When Language Fails

„In Wahrheit gehört die Geschichte nicht uns, sondern wir gehören ihr. Lange bevor wir uns durch Selbstprüfung verstehen, verstehen wir uns auf selbstverständliche Weise in Familie, Gesellschaft und Staat, in denen wir leben. Der Schwerpunkt der Subjektivität ist ein verzerrender Spiegel. Das Selbstbewußtsein des Individuums ist nur ein Flackern im geschlossenen Kreislauf des geschichtlichen Lebens. Darum sind die Vorurteile des einzelnen weit mehr als seine Urteile die geschichtliche Wirklichkeit seines Seins."

'History does not belong to us; we belong to it. Long before we understand ourselves through self-examination, we understand ourselves in a self-evident way in the family, society, and state in which we live. The centre of gravity of subjectivity is a distorting mirror. The self-consciousness of the individual is only a flickering in the closed circuit of historical life. That is why the prejudices of the individual, far more than his judgments, constitute the historical reality of his being.'

— Hans-Georg Gadamer, *Wahrheit und Methode* (1960)

When Language Fails

Preface

THIS BOOK DOES NOT OFFER A THEORY OF EVERYTHING, NOR DOES it pretend to repair what it disassembles. It begins from a more modest, and more corrosive, observation: that language routinely fails us precisely where we most insist on its authority.

Modern intellectual life is built on an unspoken confidence that our words, models, classifications, and abstractions are doing the work we think they are doing. That confidence underwrites our moral claims, our political arguments, our institutional designs, and our technological ambitions. Yet again and again, when pressure is applied – when disagreement hardens, when systems scale, when stakes rise – language fractures. Concepts blur. Definitions metastasise. Arguments talk past one another while insisting on their own clarity.

This book is an attempt to trace that failure without rushing to resolve it.

The claim is not that language is useless, nor that truth is illusory, nor that 'anything goes'. Those are caricatures produced by readers who mistake diagnosis for nihilism and uncertainty for licence. The claim is narrower and more uncomfortable: that language has domains of functional sufficiency, and that many of our most confident claims are made well beyond them.

Rather than proposing a single grand framework, the chapters that follow examine patterns of breakdown – recurring zones where linguistic precision decays, where abstraction outruns grounding, and where inherited conceptual machinery continues to operate long after its conditions of success have vanished. Some of these failures are philosophical, some institutional, some technological. Many are cultural. All are familiar, even if rarely named.

The structure of the book reflects this orientation. It moves from diagnosis to formalisation, from examples to implications, without promising closure. Where orthodox approaches would seek reconstruction, this work is content with dis-integration: taking apart what no longer holds, and resisting the reflex to rebuild prematurely. Ambiguity is not treated as a defect to be eliminated, but as a signal – often the most honest one available – that we are operating at the limits of articulation.

Readers looking for prescriptive ethics, political programmes, or totalising solutions will not find them here. What they will find, instead, is a set of tools for noticing when language is being asked to do work it cannot perform, and for recognising how much damage is done by pretending otherwise.

If the book succeeds, it may not persuade so much as recalibrate. It aims to make certain arguments harder to make in good faith, certain assumptions harder to maintain unexamined, and certain forms of certainty feel increasingly implausible. That is enough.

The work remains incomplete by design. Any attempt to finalise it would contradict its central thesis. Language does not fail once and for all; it fails situationally, repeatedly, and often productively. This book is offered in that spirit: not as an endpoint, but as a companion to ongoing intellectual discomfort.

NB: Since drafting this manuscript I have published essays that support the position in it. Rather than shoehorn them in here, instead I ask that you review the references listed at the back of this book. In particular, I might have cited the legibility of James C Scott (Illegible Futures) or the fMRI work of Ev Fedorenko (Language as Interface).

In this book I reference the work of Lakoff, Haidt, Gray, and Greene, but I discovered that Thomas Sowell (Grammatical Failure) came to similar conclusions from a different vector.

— Bry, Feb 2026

Abstract

CONTEMPORARY MORAL AND POLITICAL DISCOURSE IS MARKED BY A peculiar frustration: disputes persist even after factual clarification, legal process, and good-faith argumentation have been exhausted. Competing parties frequently agree on what happened, acknowledge that harm occurred, and yet remain irreconcilably divided over whether justice has been served. This persistence is routinely attributed to misinformation, bad faith, or affective polarisation. Such diagnoses are comforting. They are also often wrong.

This paper advances a different claim. Certain conflicts are not primarily epistemic or semantic in nature, but ontological. They arise from incompatible orientations that structure how agents register salience, threat, authority, autonomy, and legitimacy. These orientations are genealogically shaped through enculturation, institutions, and languaged traditions, yet operationally they function prior to linguistic articulation: salience fires before reasons are narrated. Moral vocabulary enters downstream, tasked with reconciling commitments that were never shared.

From this perspective, the instability of concepts such as justice is not the primary problem but a symptom. Justice belongs to a class of *Contestables* (in Gallie's sense): action-authorising terms that appear determinate whilst remaining untethered from shared reference under ontological plurality. Appeals to clearer definitions, better process, or shared values therefore misfire. They presume a common ontological ground that does not, in fact, exist.

When institutions are nevertheless required to act, they cannot adjudicate between ontologies. They can only select. Courts, juries, regulatory bodies, and enforcement agencies collapse plural interpretations into a single outcome. That outcome is necessarily experienced as legitimate by those whose orientation it instantiates, and as injustice by those whose orientation it negates. No procedural refinement can eliminate this asymmetry. At best, procedure dampens variance, distributes loss, and increases tolerability.

Crucially, the selection itself is constrained but underdetermined. Even within formal structures, human judgment, discretion, mood, confidence, fear, and narrative framing play a decisive role. Following Keynes, this irreducible contingency may be described as animal spirits. In formal terms, institutional outcomes are sampled from a constrained space of possibilities, but the reaction topology remains structurally predictable regardless of which branch is taken.

The consequence is stark but clarifying: outrage is not evidence that a system has failed to deliver justice; it is evidence that plural ontological orientations have been forced through a single decision point. Where semantic reconciliation is structurally unavailable, exogenous power is the dominant near-term mediator. Power does not resolve the conflict; it pauses it and stabilises meaning sufficiently for coordination to continue.

This analysis does not deny the reality of harm, the importance of law, or the necessity of institutions. Nor does it lapse into nihilism or indifference. Rather, it reframes the problem. In ontologically plural environments, the task is not moral convergence but maintenance: containing collision, resisting premature coherence, and designing institutions that minimise catastrophic failure rather than promising final resolution.

The argument developed here predates any particular event. Its value lies precisely in its predictive capacity. Given plural ontologies, untethered contestables, and institutions that must act, the pattern of reaction is invariant. The surface details change; the structure does not.

What follows is not a proposal for reconciliation. It is a diagnosis of why reconciliation is so often a category error, and why pretending otherwise is making things worse.

Author's Note on Position

THIS MANUSCRIPT DOES NOT CLAIM AN ONTOLOGICALLY NEUTRAL standpoint. It is written from within a particular set of methodological and temperamental leanings: scepticism that high-complexity moral and political conflict is primarily epistemic (fixable by more information), semantic (fixable by better definitions), or procedural (fixable by deliberative refinement). It treats persistent disagreement as a structural feature of plural societies rather than an anomaly attributable solely to ignorance or bad faith.

This disclosure is not an appeal for indulgence or a claim to privileged access. It is included because the argument itself insists that analyses of moral and political conflict are always produced from within ontological orientations. The claims that follow stand or fall on explanatory adequacy: whether the proposed structure better predicts and clarifies recurring patterns of non-convergence under conditions where factual convergence and procedural integrity are present.

These fault-lines are repeatedly documented across independent literatures, including:

- moral psychology (e.g. moral foundations, dyadic harm models),
- cultural cognition and framing research,
- sociology and philosophy of science (paradigm and adequacy criteria divergence),
- legal and institutional analysis of legitimacy disputes.

The framework makes no claim that orientations are discrete, enumerable, or stable across contexts. Its claim is structural: when action-authorising judgments are required under ontological plurality, lexical overlap and semantic competence are insufficient to secure convergence.

Chapter 14 outlines empirical strategies for probing these fault-lines without reifying them into fixed categories.

When Language Fails

Table of Contents

Preface ix
Abstract xi
Author's Note on Position xiii
How to Read This Book xxi
The Persistence Problem 1
1.1 Working Thesis 1
1.2 Problem Statement 2
1.3 Scope and Limits of the Argument 3
1.4 Intellectual lineage 3
1.5 Disclaimers 5
Ontological Orientation 7
Genealogy and Operation 7
2.1 Genealogical Formation 8
2.2 Operational Priority 8
2.3 Ontological Orientation vs Belief and Value 9
2.4 Dimensional Structure 10
2.5 Ontological Plurality and Incommensurability 12
2.6 A Note on Moral Realism 13
2.7 Why Ontological Orientation Matters 13
LIH and the Presumption Gap 15
3.1 Language Effectiveness and Conceptual Complexity 15
3.2 The Presumption Gap 16
3.3 Contestables, Fluids, and the Failure of Repair 17
3.4 Why 'Better Dialogue' Makes Things Worse 17
3.5 Implications for the Persistence Problem 17
3.6 Transition: From Linguistic Failure to Power Mediation 18
Contestables: Untethered Action-Terms 21
4.1 What Makes a Contestable a Contestable 22
4.2 Structural Criteria for Contestability 22
4.3 Why Contestables Resist Stabilisation 23
4.4 Gallie Revisited (and Extended) 24
4.5 From Contestables to Institutions 24
4.6 Summary 25

Institutional Singularity 27
5.1 The Necessity of Singular Outcomes 28
5.2 Procedure as Variance Damping, Not Resolution 28
5.3 Power as Mediation, Not Corruption 29
5.4 Why Institutional Failure Is Misdiagnosed 29
5.5 Preview: Confirming Instances 30
Structural Constraint Model 33
6.1 Why Formalisation Is Necessary 33
6.2 The Intuitive Model 34
6.3 The Formal Model 35
6.4 What the Model Shows 36
6.5 Why Reducing Contingency Does Not Solve the Problem 36
6.6 What This Clarification Does – and Does Not – Claim 37
Power as Mediation 39
Hard, Soft, and Structural Stabilisation Under Ontological Plurality 39
7.1 Power as a Functional, Not Pathological, Mechanism 40
7.2 Three Forms of Power 40
7.3 Indexing Power to Semantic Failure 41
7.4 Power and the Illusion of Neutrality 42
7.5 From Mediation to Case Studies 42
Science as Confirming Instance 45
8.1 What Must Be Explained 46
8.2 Selection, Training, and the Manufacture of Ontological Homogeneity 46
8.3 Material Coupling: External Constraint as Disciplining Force 48
8.4. Worked Mini-Case: Consciousness Research as Ontological Collision Under Constraint 49
8.5 Mini-Case: IQ and the Nature–Nurture Dispute 51
8.6 Why Kuhn, Feyerabend, and Latour Trigger Hostility 52
8.7 Paradigm Shifts as Ontological Replacement 52
8.8 Persistent Scientific Controversies and the Replication Crisis . 53
8.9 Interdisciplinarity as a Controlled Ontological Collision 54
8.10 Why Scientific Convergence Cannot Simply Be Exported to Politics 55
8.11 Summary: Science Confirms the Mechanism 55

Policing as Confirming Instance ... 59
9.1 Selection and Acculturation as Ontological Engineering ... 60
9.2 The Officer/Civilian Binary and Epistemic Asymmetry ... 61
9.4 Why Reform Targets Miss the Mark (Without Being Useless). 63
9.5 Predictable Patterns of Outrage ... 64
9.6 Structural Isomorphism with Science ... 65
9.7 Maintenance, Not Resolution ... 65
9.8 Summary ... 66
Interlude: Police Discretion and Jury Adjudication as Temporal Variants ... 66
Interpretive Note for Isomorphic Table for Science and Policing Claims ... 68
Rational Convergence and Its Discontents: Rawls, Habermas, and the Liberal Repair Fantasy ... 73
10.1 Rawls: Convergence by Abstraction ... 73
10.2 Habermas: Convergence by Communication ... 75
10.3 The Shared Assumption: Language as Primary Mediator ... 76
10.4 From Resolution to Maintenance ... 77
From Diagnosis to Design: Why Maintenance Replaces Resolution ... 79
Maintenance Over Resolution ... 85
12.1 Resolution as a Category Error ... 85
12.2 Maintenance Defined ... 86
12.3 Design Levers for Maintenance ... 86
12.4 Why Maintenance Is Not Conservatism ... 88
12.5 Design Failure Modes ... 89
12.6 Transition ... 89
Legal Verdicts and the Invariance of Outrage ... 91
13.1 Step 0: Factual Convergence Is Not the Problem ... 91
13.2 Contestables at the Centre of Legal Judgment ... 92
13.3 Ontological Dimensions Activated ... 93
13.4 Institutional Singularity and Outcome Selection ... 94
13.5 Justice Evaluation Is Deterministic Given Ontology ... 95
13.6 Why Procedural Appeals Fail ... 95
13.7 The Role of Power, Explicit and Implicit ... 96
13.8 Why Reform Cycles Stall ... 96
13.9 Verdicts as Maintenance, Not Resolution ... 96

13.10 Pattern Across Cases: Outcome Invariance and Asymmetric Outrage 97
13.11 Structural Invariance Across Outcome 99
Methodology and Research Programme 101
14.1 What Is (and Is Not) Being Claimed 102
14.2 Behavioural Proxies for Ontological Orientation 103
14.3 Narrative Elicitation and Salience Mapping 103
14.4 Translation Stress Tests 104
14.5 Triangulation Across Methods 105
14.6 Falsifiability and Disconfirmation Conditions 105
14.7 Implications for Institutional Research 106
14.8 Summary 106
Limits, Reflexivity, and Ontological Disclosure 109
15.1 This Is Not a View from Nowhere 109
15.2 Why This Is Not Relativism in the Pejorative Sense 110
15.3 Nor Is This Quietism 111
15.4 Moral Realism as an Ontological Vector 111
15.5 Why Science Is Not a Counterexample Revisited 112
15.6 What This Framework Cannot Do 112
15.7 Why Strengthens, Not Weakens, the Argument 113
15.8 The Closing Claim 113
When Language Fails: A Closing Argument 115
16.1 The Enlightenment Promise, Reconsidered 115
16.2 Why Better Arguments Fail Predictably 116
16.3 Institutions as Collapse Mechanisms 116
16.4 Power Without Romance 117
16.5 What This Framework Offers Instead 117
16.6 The Final Provocation 117
Appendix A-121
Empirical Anchors, Scope Conditions, and Disconfirmation Criteria A-121
A0. Purpose and Status of This Appendix A-121
A1. Pre-Verbal Salience and Moral Judgment A-122
A2. Persistence After Factual Convergence A-123
A3. Transparency and Body-Camera Effects A-124
A4. Scientific Convergence as Engineered Homogeneity A-125
A.5 Scope Conditions: When the Ontological Model Applies – and When It Doesn't A-126

A6. Translation Stress and Cross-Orientation Failure A-127
A7. Illustrative Toy Design: Translation Stress Under Ontological Plurality A-127
Interpretive Note. A-129
Closing Note A-129
Glossary of Terms G-130
Select Bibliography B-133
I. Ontological Orientation, Pre-Verbal Judgment, and Moral Psychology B-133
II. Language, Contestation, and Conceptual Indeterminacy.. B-133
III. Language Insufficiency, Framing, and the Limits of Semantic Repair B-134
IV. Science, Incommensurability, and Engineered Convergence B-134
V. Law, Policing, and Institutional Judgment B-134
VI. Liberal Proceduralism and Its Scope Conditions B-135
VII. Power, Institutions, and Structural Mediation B-135
VIII. Design, Pluralism, and Maintenance B-135
IX. Author's Prior Work and Related Frameworks B-135
Index I-137

When Language Fails

How to Read This Book

THIS BOOK IS NOT A POLEMIC AGAINST REASON, DIALOGUE, science, law, or liberal institutions. Nor is it a brief for relativism, cynicism, or political quietism. It is a structural diagnosis of a recurrent failure mode in plural societies: situations in which disagreement persists despite factual clarification, procedural integrity, and good-faith exchange.

Readers should therefore resist several common but misleading expectations.

This Is Not an Argument About Bad Faith or Irrationality

The analysis does not depend on actors being ignorant, dishonest, biased, or malicious – though such features may of course be present in particular cases. The claim is structural: even under conditions of informational symmetry, procedural fairness, and sincere engagement, certain conflicts persist. Where this happens reliably, appeals to better facts or better motives mislocate the problem.

The framework treats moral judgment as competent, not defective – competent relative to an agent's ontological orientation.

This Is Not a Semantic Dispute

Much of the argument turns on concepts that appear familiar – justice, legitimacy, reasonable force, harm. These terms are not analysed here as merely vague or poorly defined. They are treated as Contestables: action-authorising concepts that function effectively within orientations whilst lacking shared ontological grounding across them.

Accordingly, readers should not expect semantic clarification to do the explanatory work. Language is the site where conflict appears, not necessarily where it originates.

The Central Claims Are Descriptive Before They Are Normative

The manuscript first asks what is happening before asking what ought to be done. Chapters 1–10 are primarily diagnostic: they aim to explain why certain conflicts predictably resist resolution. Only later does the book turn to institutional implications, and even then the normative ambition is deliberately constrained.

The proposed shift from resolution to maintenance should be read as a design recommendation under acknowledged constraints, not as a moral endorsement of existing outcomes.

Case Studies Are Confirming Instances, Not Universal Templates

The analyses of science, policing, and legal verdicts are not offered as exhaustive or paradigmatic of all disagreement. They are chosen because they allow the same structural mechanism to be observed under different conditions of power, coercion, and material constraint.

Readers should attend less to surface differences between cases than to the recurring pattern: convergence where ontological variance is reduced and disciplined, fracture where it is not.

The Formal Model Clarifies Dependencies; It Does Not Predict Outcomes

The minimal formalism introduced in Chapter 6 is not a predictive engine. It serves to make explicit what depends on what: how evaluative judgments track ontological orientation given an institutional selection, and why institutional outputs are underdetermined relative to plural inputs.

Readers uninterested in formal representation can safely skim this chapter without loss of argumentative continuity.

The Methodology Is a Research Programme, Not a Protocol

Chapter 14 and the empirical appendix outline how claims about ontological orientation could be investigated without presupposing fixed group taxonomies or treating disagreement as error. These sections are not experimental recipes. They specify scope conditions, diagnostic strategies, and disconfirmation criteria.

The absence of large-N data here is intentional. The framework is offered as a lens to organise and interpret existing findings, and as a guide for future inquiry – not as a completed empirical programme.

Reflexivity Is a Feature, Not a Defect

The author's ontological orientation is disclosed not to immunise the argument from critique, but to make its standpoint explicit. The framework does not claim a privileged view from nowhere. Its ambition is more modest and more demanding: to describe the conditions under which no such view is available, yet decisions must still be made.

Reading Strategy

Readers encountering resistance or frustration should note where it arises. Persistent disagreement with the framework may itself be diagnostic. The aim of the book is not to secure assent, but to make disagreement legible – especially where disagreement survives explanation.

If the argument succeeds, it will not persuade everyone. It will, however, make clear why persuasion was never the appropriate expectation.

1

The Persistence Problem

1.1 Working Thesis

In plural societies, moral and political conflict persists not primarily because of disagreement over facts, values, or semantics, but because of structurally incompatible ontological orientations. These orientations are genealogically shaped through culture, institutions, and languaged traditions, yet operationally they function pre-verbally in the assignment of salience – what registers as authority, autonomy, threat, harm, or legitimacy.[1]

Where such orientations collide, key action-authorising terms (for example justice, legitimacy, or reasonable force) function as untethered *Contestables* in Gallie's sense: they appear determinate whilst lacking shared ontological reference.[2] Institutions, however, are singularity machines.[3] They

1 On salience as pre-propositional and action-guiding, see Pierre Bourdieu, *Outline of a Theory of Practice* (1977), esp. the discussion of habitus as structuring perception prior to deliberation. For contemporary cognitive framing of salience assignment, see George Lakoff, *Moral Politics* (1996; rev. ed. 2016).

2 W. B. Gallie, 'Essentially Contested Concepts', *Proceedings of the Aristotelian Society* 56 (1956): 167–198. Gallie's account explains persistent disagreement despite apparent shared usage, though it does not address institutional decision constraints under plurality.

3 For the necessity of determinate outputs under institutional conditions, see Niklas Luhmann, *Law as a Social System* (2004), on decision closure and system reproduction. Compare with Carl Schmitt, *Political Theology* (1922), for the irreducibility of decision under indeterminacy, though Schmitt's theological commitments are not retained here.

must output one outcome. Any such outcome therefore instantiates one ontological orientation over others.

Settlement is achieved not through semantic convergence but chiefly through exogenous power – hard, soft, or structural – modulated by contingent human judgment ('animal spirits')[4] and institutional selection effects. Asymmetric outrage is thus not a failure of process but a predictable structural invariant.[5] Procedure can dampen variance and distribute loss; it cannot reconcile ontological plurality.

That is core. Everything else in this manuscript is elaboration, illustration, or defence.

1.2 Problem Statement

Certain moral and political conflicts persist after factual clarification, procedural integrity, and good-faith exchange. This manuscript treats such persistence as diagnostic: not a sign of irrationality or bad faith, but a marker of ontological collision rather than merely epistemic disagreement.[6]

It proposes a set of observable markers – persistence after clarification, escalation under contact, translation failure, asymmetric harm recognition – and argues that standard remedies misapply tools suited to lower-complexity domains.[7] Where disagreement is ontological rather than semantic, attempts at repair through better argument, clearer definitions, or increased dialogue predictably fail.

---

4 On power as constitutive rather than merely distortive of political outcomes, see Michel Foucault, *Society Must Be Defended* (1975–76 lectures). For 'animal spirits' as a stabilising but non-rational residue in collective judgment, see John Maynard Keynes, *The General Theory of Employment,* Interest and Money (1936), ch. 12.

5 The idea that persistence signals category error rather than argumentative failure parallels Ludwig Wittgenstein, *Philosophical Investigations* (1953), §§109–133, though Wittgenstein does not extend this diagnosis to institutional design or moral conflict.

6 For translation failure without irrationality, see Thomas Kuhn, *The Structure of Scientific Revolutions* (1962), on incommensurability. The present argument generalises this phenomenon beyond scientific theory change to moral and political evaluation.

7 On the systematic failure of argument to change moral judgments, see Jonathan Haidt, *The Righteous Mind* (2012). Haidt's own normative optimism about dialogue is treated here as empirically unsupported given his descriptive findings.

1.3 Scope and Limits of the Argument

This framework is not a general theory of disagreement. It does not apply to low-stakes disputes, to domains governed by stable technical criteria, or to conflicts where incentives, information asymmetries, or strategic behaviour plausibly explain persistence. In such cases, standard epistemic, economic, or game-theoretic accounts remain sufficient and appropriate. The model advanced here is indexed, not totalising: it applies most forcefully to high-salience, identity-loaded, action-authorising conflicts in which evaluative concepts carry institutional force and disagreement persists despite factual convergence and procedural integrity. Where ontological variance is low, shared background orientation is strong, or action stakes are limited, language, evidence, and deliberation often do succeed. The claim is not that all disagreement is ontological, but that some structurally important failures of convergence cannot be adequately explained without recognising ontological plurality as an operative constraint.

1.4 Intellectual lineage

This project builds directly on empirical moral psychology and cognitive linguistics, particularly the work of George Lakoff, Jonathan Haidt, Kurt Gray, and Joshua Greene, whose combined findings establish a now well-supported claim: moral judgment is structured prior to conscious reasoning and linguistic articulation,[8] and justificatory reasoning typically operates downstream of evaluative salience rather than determining it.

These programmes converge on a shared empirical insight despite theoretical divergence. Moral evaluation is fast, affectively mediated, and structured by cognitive architectures that operate below the level of propositional belief. Individuals routinely experience moral judgments as immediate and obvious, and only subsequently supply reasons that render those judgments intelligible within shared linguistic frameworks.

Where this manuscript departs is not in rejecting these findings, but in following them to their institutional implications.

8 Empirical moral psychology consistently shows that moral judgment is fast, affectively mediated, and structured prior to conscious reasoning or linguistic articulation. See Jonathan Haidt, *The Righteous Mind* (2012); Joshua Greene, *Moral Tribes* (2013); Kurt Gray, Liane Young, and Adam Waytz (2012); George Lakoff, *Moral Politics* (1996/2016).

Lakoff demonstrated that moral reasoning is scaffolded by deep conceptual metaphors that structure political cognition well before deliberation, most notably in the 'Strict Father' and 'Nurturant Parent' frames.[9] His later work, however, prescribes improved political framing as a remedy, implicitly treating semantic intervention as capable of producing convergence across fundamentally different moral orientations.

Haidt's moral foundations theory similarly establishes that moral intuitions arise pre-reflectively and that reasoning functions largely as post-hoc rationalisation. Yet *The Righteous Mind* ultimately returns to a project of mutual understanding and cross-partisan dialogue, implying that recognition of divergent foundations can restore deliberative equilibrium.

Gray's dyadic model of moral cognition shows that moral disagreement frequently turns on asymmetric perceptions of agency and patiency, even where factual agreement exists. Awareness of this structure, however, is offered as a corrective rather than as a constraint on what moral discourse can achieve. Bernard Williams similarly recognised the fragility of moral objectivity under conditions of plural evaluative frameworks. Yet Williams, like Gray, stops short of treating institutional outcomes as necessarily exclusionary instantiations of competing values.

Greene's dual-process account distinguishes affective and deliberative moral cognition and explicitly documents the temporal priority of emotional response. Nevertheless, his normative prescriptions favour rational override, treating pre-verbal salience as something to be resisted rather than as a structural feature with institutional consequences.

Taken together, these literatures document the architecture of moral cognition, but stop short of confronting its implications for collective decision-making under pluralism.[10] Having established that moral judgment is pre-verbally structured and only partially accessible to conscious reasoning, they nevertheless return to prescriptions – better framing, deeper dialogue, improved deliberation – that presuppose convergence conditions their own evidence destabilises.

9 Lakoff's 'Strict Father' and 'Nurturant Parent' models originate in *Moral Politics*. The critique offered here targets the implicit assumption that reframing can overcome ontological divergence rather than merely mobilise within it.

10 For deliberative optimism under pluralism, see Jürgen Habermas, *Between Facts and Norms* (1992). The present framework argues that Habermasian convergence conditions presuppose ontological alignment that cannot be assumed in high-salience conflicts.

This manuscript treats that retreat not as an oversight, but as the unresolved problem. If moral disagreement is not merely epistemic or semantic, but ontological – rooted in divergent pre-verbal orientations that structure salience, legitimacy, and harm recognition – then institutional design cannot be evaluated primarily by its capacity to produce consensus. Institutions must decide despite irreducible plurality, and moral conflict must be analysed as a structural feature of that necessity rather than as a correctable failure of discourse.

The argument that follows does not deny the value of understanding, dialogue, or transparency. It specifies their limits.

1.5 Disclaimers

This manuscript does not claim that all disagreement is ontological in kind. Many disputes are straightforwardly epistemic, interest-based, or strategic, and are often resolved by improved information, incentives, or enforcement. The present analysis is indexed to a specific class of conflicts: those that are high-stakes, identity-loaded, action-authorising, and persistent after factual clarification and procedural integrity. It is under these conditions that ontological divergence becomes dominant and semantic repair reaches its *effectiveness horizon*.

Claims of bad faith, strategic rhetoric, or interest-driven behaviour are often correct at the level of local interaction. However, they do not explain the structural persistence of disagreement across good-faith contexts, nor the invariance of asymmetric outrage across outcome directions. In the present framework, bad faith is not an alternative explanation but a predictable secondary phenomenon: once ontological misalignment renders reconciliation unavailable, strategic behaviour rationally intensifies. Interests exploit ontological fracture; they do not generate it.

Ontological Orientation

Genealogy and Operation

THIS MANUSCRIPT USES THE TERM ONTOLOGICAL ORIENTATION TO name a feature of human world-relation that is frequently gestured at but rarely stabilised. Ontological orientation refers to the pre-verbally operative structuring of salience through which agents register what matters, what threatens, what authorises, what constrains, and what counts as legitimate.[11] It is not a belief, a value, or a theory about the world. It is the condition under which beliefs, values, and theories become intelligible at all.

Ontological orientations are genealogically shaped but operationally prior. They emerge through cultural transmission, institutional training, and historically sedimented linguistic practice, yet they function beneath and before linguistic articulation. Salience fires before reasons are narrated. Evaluation precedes justification.

11 'Ontological' here does not refer to metaphysical claims about what exists, but to the pre-reflective structuring of what matters – what registers as salient, authoritative, or threatening prior to deliberation and independent of propositional endorsement. Compare Martin Heidegger's notion of *Befindlichkeit* (attunement) as a condition of intelligibility, though without Heidegger's phenomenological commitments. For orientation as a structural feature of cognition rather than content, see Hubert Dreyfus, *Being-in-the-World* (1991), on skillful coping and background intelligibility.

This distinction between genealogy and operation is central. Confusing the two has led many otherwise sophisticated accounts of moral and political disagreement to misidentify the locus of conflict.

2.1 Genealogical Formation

Ontological orientations are not innate in any strong sense. They are cultivated over time through immersion in social practices, narratives, institutions, and roles. Family structure, education, religious tradition, professional training, media environment, and political context all contribute to shaping what is experienced as obvious, dangerous, authoritative, or inviolable.

Importantly, genealogical shaping does not require explicit instruction. Much of it occurs tacitly, through habituation rather than argument. One learns not only what to think, but what to notice, what to ignore, and what to treat as non-negotiable. These dispositions are reinforced by reward, sanction, imitation, and exclusion long before they are ever verbalised.

Genealogy explains why ontological orientations cluster within professions, institutions, and subcultures.[12] It also explains why such orientations are remarkably stable over time, resistant to counter-argument, and often experienced as self-evident rather than learned.

2.2 Operational Priority

Whilst genealogically shaped, ontological orientations operate prior to language and deliberation. They are not conclusions reached through reasoning, but conditions under which reasoning takes place.

When an event occurs, agents do not first neutrally perceive it and then interpret it through values or principles. They experience it as already salient in particular ways: as threatening or benign, legitimate or suspect, accidental or intentional. Only after this pre-verbal appraisal do reasons, narratives, and justifications emerge.

This operational priority is not speculative. It is supported by extensive

12 The genealogical account here follows Michel Foucault's emphasis on how practices, institutions, and discourses shape subjects without determining them (*Discipline and Punish*, 1975; *The History of Sexuality*, Vol. 1, 1976). However, the present framework does not adopt Foucault's full archaeological–genealogical apparatus or his treatment of power/knowledge as co-constitutive. Genealogy here explains formation; it does not reduce agents to effects of discourse.

work in cognitive science, moral psychology, and neuroscience, which consistently shows that evaluative processing precedes conscious reasoning.

Deliberation typically functions to rationalise, stabilise, or communicate judgments already in motion.[13]

The practical consequence is decisive: disagreement often arises not at the level of reasons offered, but at the level of what counts as a reason in the first place.

2.3 Ontological Orientation vs Belief and Value

Ontological orientation should not be conflated with beliefs, values, or preferences.

Beliefs are propositions held to be true or false. Values are articulated commitments or ideals. Preferences are ranked choices among alternatives. Ontological orientations precede all three. They determine which propositions appear plausible,[14] which values feel compelling, and which preferences seem morally or practically permissible.

Two agents may share many explicit beliefs and still diverge sharply in judgment because their ontological orientations weight salience differently. Conversely, agents may disagree vociferously at the level of belief whilst remaining aligned ontologically, allowing for eventual convergence once factual disputes are resolved.

This distinction explains why some disagreements dissolve with evidence whilst others persist indefinitely despite shared facts and good faith.

2.4 Dimensional Structure

13 See Chapter 1, fn. 8, for representative findings. For neuroscientific evidence of affective processing preceding conscious evaluation, see Antonio Damasio, *Descartes' Error* (1994), and Joseph LeDoux, *The Emotional Brain* (1996). The timing claim is robust across methodologies: fMRI studies (Greene et al., 2001), response-time experiments (Haidt, 2001), and priming studies (Bargh & Chartrand, 1999) all confirm that evaluative salience precedes articulated reasoning.

14 This priority claim is structural, not temporal. Ontological orientation does not causally precede belief formation in developmental time, but operates as a condition of intelligibility for beliefs. The distinction parallels Wilfrid Sellars' contrast between the 'manifest image' and the 'space of reasons' (*Philosophy and the Scientific Image of Man*, 1962), though Sellars' project aimed at reconciliation rather than acknowledging irreducible plurality. For orientation as pre-propositional, see also Hubert Dreyfus and Charles Taylor, *Retrieving Realism* (2015), on engaged agency.

Ontological orientations are multidimensional. They do not reduce to a single axis such as rationality versus emotion, or individualism versus collectivism. Instead, they consist of multiple interacting dimensions along which salience, legitimacy, and action-authorisation are pre-verbally assigned and weighted.

These dimensions do not function as explicit principles or articulated values. In most cases they are neither recognised nor named by the agents who instantiate them. Disagreement arises not because parties select different answers to shared questions, but because they treat different dimensions as decisive in the first place, whilst regarding others as marginal, irrelevant, or illegitimate.

The dimensions presented below should therefore be read diagnostically, not canonically. They do not constitute a taxonomy of moral types, nor do they imply global consistency across domains. Weightings vary across individuals, cohorts, and contexts, and may shift over time. What matters structurally is not the presence of any single dimension, but the pattern of salience it exerts relative to others.

Table 1 summarises recurring ontological fault-lines along which evaluative judgment, legitimacy attribution, and institutional outcomes systematically diverge.[15]

15 The dimensional structure presented here is influenced by Jonathan Haidt's moral foundations theory (*The Righteous Mind*, 2012) and George Lakoff's metaphor analysis (*Moral Politics*, 1996/2016), but differs in two respects. First, it treats dimensions as diagnostically useful rather than empirically fixed. Second, it does not claim that dimensions are innate, universal, or stable across contexts. For multidimensional models of political orientation, see also Philip Converse, 'The Nature of Belief Systems in Mass Publics' (1964), and Shalom Schwartz on value dimensions (1992). The present framework is agnostic about whether these dimensions are discoverable universals or contingent patterns shaped by institutional and cultural history.

Table 2.1: Ontological Fault-Lines (Diagnostic, Non-Taxonomic)

The following dimensions represent recurring fault-lines along which evaluative salience, legitimacy attribution, and action-authorisation diverge. They are not exhaustive, mutually exclusive, or empirically fixed. Positions may vary by domain; the table does not imply global consistency or stable typologies.

Fault-Line	Pole A	Pole B	What Diverges Pre-Verbally
Authority Orientation	Authority-centred	Autonomy-centred	Whether legitimacy flows from hierarchy or individual agency
Harm Salience	Outcome-focused	Intent-focused	Whether harm registers by effects or mental states
Moral Jurisdiction	Universalist	Locally contained	Whether moral norms bind all others by default
Threat Sensitivity	Precautionary	Tolerant	Whether ambiguity triggers defensive action or restraint
Order vs Mercy	Order-prioritising	Mercy-prioritising	Whether stability or compassion anchors legitimacy
Rule Construal	Deontic	Contextual	Whether rules bind regardless of context
Boundary Policing	Purity-oriented	Integration-oriented	Whether boundary violation itself constitutes harm
Responsibility Attribution	Individualised	Structural	Whether blame tracks agents or systems
Temporal Moral Scope	Retrospective	Prospective	Whether justice centres on past acts or future prevention
Conflict Posture	Zero-sum	Pluralist	Whether coexistence without convergence is acceptable

Ontological fault-lines are domain-indexed rather than globally applied. Agents may treat certain classes of claims – such as religious truth, harm thresholds, dignity, or sovereignty – as universally binding, whilst regarding others as locally negotiable or procedurally mediated. Apparent inconsistency is therefore not a defect of reasoning but a feature of how moral salience is hierarchically structured across domains.

A single agent may, without experiencing contradiction, be universalist about religious command, localist about cultural practice, essentialist about biological categories, and proceduralist about political legitimacy. What appears incoherent from the outside is internally coherent once the dimensional structure of salience is made explicit.

2.5 Ontological Plurality and Incommensurability

Ontological plurality refers to the coexistence of multiple, incompatible orientations within the same social space. In such contexts, agents do not merely disagree about outcomes; they disagree about what counts as harm, authority, legitimacy, or violation.

This plurality does not imply that orientations are arbitrary or equally defensible. It implies that they are structurally incommensurable at certain levels of complexity. There is no neutral vantage point from which all orientations can be jointly adjudicated without remainder.[16]

Attempts to resolve such conflicts through better definitions, clearer communication, or increased empathy often fail not because participants are insincere or irrational, but because these strategies operate downstream of the divergence they seek to repair.

16 On incommensurability without relativism, see Thomas Kuhn, *The Structure of Scientific Revolutions* (1962), especially the postscript to the second edition (1970), where Kuhn clarifies that incommensurability does not entail incomparability or irrationality. See also Paul Feyerabend, *Against Method* (1975), and Richard Rorty, *Philosophy and the Mirror of Nature* (1979), on the absence of a neutral framework for adjudication. The present claim is narrower: incommensurability arises under plural ontological orientation, not universally. Where ontological variance is low, adjudication remains possible.

2.6 A Note on Moral Realism

The structural thesis advanced here is compatible with moral realism. Even if moral properties exist independently of human cognition, their recognition, prioritisation, and institutional instantiation remain mediated by ontological orientation. Realism about moral facts does not entail convergence in moral judgment, any more than realism about physical facts guarantees agreement under conditions of limited access, asymmetric salience, or interpretive constraint.

One may consistently hold that moral truths exist whilst acknowledging that agents, institutions, and societies will differ in how those truths are apprehended, weighted, and enacted. Ontological orientation governs access, not ontology itself.

This accommodation is not a concession. It clarifies the target of the argument. The problem addressed in this manuscript is not whether moral facts exist, but why persistent disagreement and institutional conflict remain predictable even if they do.

2.7 Why Ontological Orientation Matters

By distinguishing genealogy from operation, and by treating ontological orientation as pre-verbally operative, we gain a clearer account of why moral and political disagreement persists beyond the reach of reasoned discourse.

Disagreement is not merely about facts or values. It is about the structures through which facts become salient and values acquire force.

The chapters that follow build on this foundation. First, by showing how language fails to stabilise meaning under these conditions; then by formalising the resulting constraints on institutions; and finally by examining how power mediates where semantic reconciliation is unavailable.

3

LIH and the Presumption Gap

THE ARGUMENT ADVANCED IN THIS MANUSCRIPT PRESUPPOSES A failure mode that is often misdiagnosed as rhetorical incompetence or moral stubbornness. That failure mode is linguistic rather than psychological, and structural rather than accidental. To make this explicit, this chapter situates the analysis within the Language Insufficiency Hypothesis (LIH): the claim that as conceptual complexity increases, the effectiveness of language decreases, even as speakers' confidence in their communicative success often remains high.[1]

This divergence between actual and perceived communicative effectiveness is central. It explains not only why certain disputes fail to resolve, but why attempts at clarification, definition, and dialogue frequently intensify conflict once a threshold of complexity is crossed.

3.1 Language Effectiveness and Conceptual Complexity

At low levels of complexity, language performs well. Referential terms anchored to shared observables, stable procedures, or tightly constrained practices exhibit high effectiveness. Disagreement in such domains is typically resolvable through clarification, additional information, or procedural appeal.

1 LIH does not treat linguistic failure as psychological deficit or rhetorical error. It describes a structural divergence between conceptual load and communicative effectiveness that arises independently of speaker competence or intent.

As abstraction increases, however, language loses traction. Terms become less directly tethered to shared experience and more dependent on background assumptions, evaluative weightings, and unarticulated commitments. Crucially, this degradation is gradual rather than abrupt. Speakers remain fluent, grammatically competent, and rhetorically confident long after mutual intelligibility has begun to erode.

LIH formalises this intuition: language effectiveness declines as conceptual load increases, but perceived effectiveness does not decline at the same rate. Speakers continue to experience themselves as '*making sense*', even as their utterances become increasingly underdetermined relative to their interlocutors' ontological frameworks.

3.2 The Presumption Gap

The presumption gap names the space between actual communicative effectiveness and presumed communicative success.[2] Within this gap, participants believe they are clarifying positions when in fact they are projecting ontological commitments that cannot be shared.

This gap explains a familiar pattern: escalation through explanation. When initial disagreement persists, speakers respond not by questioning the limits of language, but by increasing semantic density. Definitions are sharpened, arguments refined, examples multiplied. Each move is locally rational. Collectively, they produce mutual frustration.

The reason is not bad faith or incompetence. It is structural miscalibration. Once a dispute occupies the boundary between *Contestables* and *Fluids* – terms that appear determinate whilst lacking shared ontological anchoring – additional linguistic effort does not repair meaning.[3] It amplifies divergence by forcing each party to articulate commitments the other cannot recognise as salient.

2 'Presumption' is used descriptively rather than normatively. It refers to the functional necessity of acting under conditions where linguistic articulation exceeds shared ontological grounding, not to arrogance, bad faith, or epistemic vice.

3 The use of 'Contestables' here builds on W. B. Gallie's account of essentially contested concepts, but extends it to cases where contestation persists because terms function without shared ontological anchoring rather than because of evaluative disagreement alone.

3.3 Contestables, Fluids, and the Failure of Repair

The class of terms most vulnerable to this failure are those that authorise action whilst concealing their ontological dependence. Words such as justice, legitimacy, reasonable force, or harm function as if they were stable referents.[4] In practice, their application depends on prior salience assignments that are not linguistically negotiable.

LIH predicts that disputes involving such terms will exhibit three features:

1. Persistence after clarification: disagreement remains even when factual disagreement is resolved.
2. Escalation under dialogue: increased engagement intensifies rather than alleviates conflict.
3. Asymmetric incomprehension: each side experiences the other as irrational, dishonest, or morally defective.

These are not pathologies of discourse. They are signatures of language operating beyond its effective horizon.

3.4 Why 'Better Dialogue' Makes Things Worse

Much contemporary political and moral theory treats dialogue as an unqualified good. The implicit assumption is that misunderstanding is semantic and therefore reparable. LIH complicates this picture.

Where ontological orientations diverge, dialogue often increases the presumption gap. Participants mistake fluency for convergence and coherence for shared grounding. The result is a familiar but poorly theorised phenomenon: the sense that '*we are talking past each other*', coupled with the conviction that the fault lies with the other party's unwillingness to listen.

From the LIH perspective, this is predictable. Language has not failed because it is imprecise. It has failed because it is being asked to do work – ontological alignment – that it cannot perform.

3.5 Implications for the Persistence Problem

LIH supplies a crucial bridge between individual cognition and institutional conflict. It explains why moral and political disputes so often survive exhaustive argumentation, and why appeals to reason, empathy, or shared values fail precisely where they are most urgently deployed.

4 These examples are illustrative rather than exhaustive. The mechanism applies to any term that authorises action whilst presupposing shared evaluative grounding.

The persistence problem, introduced in Chapter 1, is therefore not merely a problem of plural values or competing interests. It is a problem of linguistic overreach. Institutions, reformers, and theorists continue to rely on semantic tools in domains where semantic repair is structurally unavailable.

This misapplication does not merely fail to resolve conflict. It exacerbates it by widening the presumption gap and entrenching ontological asymmetry.

3.6 Transition: From Linguistic Failure to Power Mediation

If language cannot reconcile *Contestables* under conditions of ontological plurality, something else must mediate coordination. That mediator is not consensus but power. The next chapter makes this explicit.

Where language reaches its effectiveness horizon, institutions stabilise meaning through coercion, norm-setting, and structural constraint. Power does not solve the ontological problem. It suspends it long enough for collective action to proceed.

Understanding this transition – from linguistic failure to power mediation – is essential for making sense of both scientific convergence and its apparent counterexamples. It is to that analysis that the manuscript now turns.

Contestables: Untethered Action-Terms

Not all disagreement is created equal. Some disputes dissolve with clarification; others metastasise under it. The difference does not lie primarily in temperament, sincerity, or intelligence, but in the kind of concepts at issue. This chapter isolates a class of terms that reliably resist semantic stabilisation under conditions of ontological plurality. These are referred to here as *Contestables*.

The term draws on W.B. Gallie's notion of essentially contested concepts, but with a shift in emphasis.[1] Gallie treated contestation as a feature of certain evaluative concepts embedded in complex social practices. The present analysis agrees with the diagnosis but relocates the cause. Contestation is not essential because these concepts are vague, morally rich, or politically charged. It is essential because, under plural ontological orientation, they lack a shared tether to what counts as salient, authoritative, or legitimate.

Contestables are not merely disputed. They are untethered.[2]

1 See W. B. Gallie, 'Essentially Contested Concepts' (1956). Gallie treated contestation as a feature of evaluative concepts embedded in complex social practices. The present account accepts the descriptive insight but relocates the source of persistence from evaluative disagreement to the absence of shared ontological anchoring under plural orientation.

2 'Untethered' indicates the absence of a shared ontological reference that would stabilise application, not mere vagueness or semantic openness. *Contestables* remain linguistically fluent and institutionally operative despite lacking such tethering.

4.1 What Makes a Contestable a Contestable

A *Contestable* is an action-authorising term whose apparent determinacy conceals the absence of shared ontological reference. Such terms present themselves as if they name a stable property or standard, but in practice they function as projection surfaces for incompatible orientations.

When invoked, *Contestables* do not merely describe. They justify, permit, prohibit, or compel. They are the terms through which institutions act, punish, exclude, or legitimate. This is why their instability matters.

To clarify the terrain, it is useful to distinguish *Contestables* from two adjacent classes:

Invariants: terms that remain tightly tethered to shared observables, procedures, or operational definitions. Their application can be disputed, but disagreement is typically resolvable through clarification or appeal to agreed standards.

Ineffables: experiences or states that resist linguistic capture altogether. These do not authorise action in institutional settings and therefore do not generate the same kind of conflict.

Contestables sit between these poles. They are linguistically fluent, institutionally indispensable, and ontologically underdetermined.

4.2 Structural Criteria for Contestability

Contestability is not a matter of opinion or rhetorical heat. It is diagnosable. A term functions as a *Contestable* to the extent that it satisfies the following structural criteria. These criteria are not individually sufficient, but the presence of several is predictive.

4.2.1. Distance from Observables

The term cannot be grounded in shared perceptual reference, direct measurement, or uncontroversial procedure. Its application depends on interpretation rather than detection.

Examples include justice, legitimacy, or reasonable force.[3] By contrast, speed, temperature, or blood alcohol concentration are tightly tethered to observables, even when thresholds are debated.

3 These examples are illustrative rather than exhaustive. Any term that authorises action whilst presupposing shared evaluative grounding may function as a *Contestable* under conditions of ontological plurality.

4.2.2. Dependence on Thick Ethical Concepts

The term presupposes background notions such as intent, desert, proportionality, culpability, or authority. These notions are themselves ontologically indexed and cannot be specified without invoking prior commitments.

Attempts to 'define' such terms typically smuggle in the very assumptions under dispute.

4.2.3. Identity-Load-Bearing Function

Contestation of the term threatens self-conception, group legitimacy, or moral standing. To lose the argument is not merely to be mistaken, but to be discredited as an agent, citizen, or member of a moral community.

This is why disputes over *Contestables* so readily escalate. What is at stake is not only policy or outcome, but recognition.

4.2.4. Action-Authorising Role

The term is invoked to justify coercive, exclusionary, or irreversible action. It licenses arrest, punishment, removal, enforcement, or denial of access.

This criterion is crucial. *Contestables* matter because institutions must act, not merely describe. Where action is required, semantic underdetermination becomes operationally explosive.

4.2.5. Temporal and Modal Loading

The term projects necessity rather than description. It answers not only what is, but what must be done, what should have happened, or what is required now. It is inherently forward-looking and norm-binding.

This modal force gives *Contestables* their urgency and their volatility.

4.3 Why Contestables Resist Stabilisation

Under ontological plurality, *Contestables* lack a shared anchoring point. Different cohorts apply them sincerely, competently, and with full linguistic fluency – yet reach incompatible conclusions. This is not because the term is poorly defined, but because its application depends on salience assignments that are not linguistically accessible.

Language can circulate these terms. It cannot reconcile the orientations that give them force.

This explains why semantic repair fails.[4] Refining definitions, adding qualifiers, or appealing to precedent does not stabilise meaning. It merely shifts the site of contestation upstream or downstream, often intensifying the dispute.

In this sense, *Contestables* mark the effectiveness horizon of language. They are where linguistic confidence remains high even as communicative traction collapses.

4.4 Gallie Revisited (and Extended)

Gallie was right to observe that certain concepts remain contested even among competent users acting in good faith. Where he stopped was at plural description. The present account extends his insight by identifying the structural conditions under which contestation becomes invariant.

Contestables are not contested because communities value different exemplars or traditions. They are contested because, under plural ontological orientation, there is no shared answer to what counts as harm, authority, or legitimacy in the first place.

This relocation matters. It explains why contestation persists even when participants acknowledge each other's sincerity, competence, and moral seriousness. The disagreement is not about application within a shared framework. It is about which framework is operative at all.

4.5 From Contestables to Institutions

Contestables become politically and morally dangerous when institutions must decide. Courts, regulators, police, and administrative bodies cannot suspend action until ontological alignment is achieved. They must collapse plural interpretations into a single outcome.

When this occurs, the selected interpretation is experienced as justice by those whose orientation it instantiates, and as injustice by those whose orientation it negates. This asymmetry is not a procedural failure. It is a structural consequence of using untethered action-terms under conditions of plurality.

The next chapter formalises this constraint. The chapter after that explains how institutions survive it.

---

4 Refining definitions, adding qualifiers, or appealing to precedent presupposes shared criteria of relevance. Where ontological orientation diverges, such criteria are not jointly available, rendering semantic repair structurally ineffective rather than merely incomplete.

4.6 Summary

Contestables are not vague terms awaiting clearer definition. They are action-authorising concepts whose apparent stability conceals a lack of shared ontological tethering. Under plural orientation, they cannot be semantically reconciled. They can only be instantiated.

Recognising this does not resolve conflict. It clarifies why resolution so often proves to be a category error – and why the persistence of disagreement is not an anomaly, but a diagnostic signal.

Institutional Singularity

MODERN INSTITUTIONS ARE FREQUENTLY DESCRIBED AS NEUTRAL arbiters: mechanisms designed to process plural inputs through shared procedures and arrive at legitimate outcomes. This description is accurate as far as it goes – but it obscures a structural constraint that becomes decisive under conditions of ontological plurality.

Institutions do not merely coordinate disagreement. They must terminate it.[1]

Image 5.1: Ontological Orientation
Illustrates the structural condition that gives rise to institutional singularity.

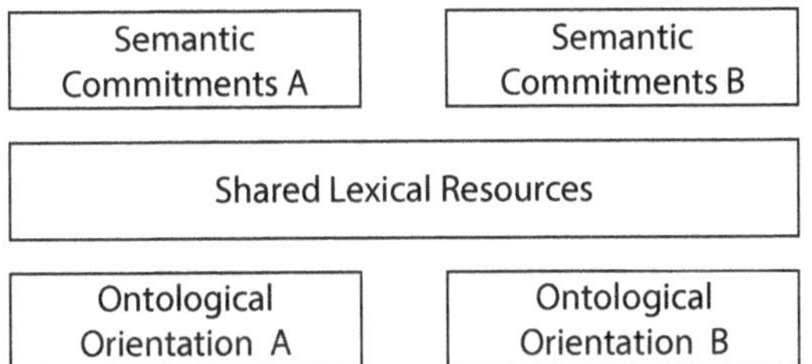

1 On decision-closure as a constitutive feature of institutions, see Niklas Luhmann, Law as a Social System (2004), on the necessity of determinate outputs for system reproduction. Compare Carl Schmitt, Political Theology (1922), on the irreducibility of decision under conditions of indeterminacy, abstracted here from Schmitt's theological and authoritarian commitments.

5.1 The Necessity of Singular Outcomes

Unlike informal discourse, institutions cannot remain indeterminate. Courts must acquit or convict. Regulatory agencies must approve or deny. Scientific bodies must publish or reject. Elections must yield a winner. Even where procedures are iterative or revisable, each iteration requires a determinate output. This requirement is not ideological. It is functional. Institutions exist to act.

Where ontological orientations diverge, however, no available outcome can be neutral. Each possible decision instantiates one evaluative configuration rather than another – authorising one conception of harm, responsibility, legitimacy, or proportionality over its competitors. The institution therefore becomes what can be called a singularity machine: a system that collapses plural interpretations into a single binding result.[2] This collapse is unavoidable. It is not a failure of design.

5.2 Procedure as Variance Damping, Not Resolution

Procedural safeguards – due process, evidentiary standards, transparency requirements, deliberative rules – play a crucial role in institutional legitimacy.

They can:

- expand agreement over descriptive facts,
- constrain arbitrary discretion,
- distribute losses more predictably,
- and reduce perceptions of caprice or bias.

What they cannot do is eliminate ontological asymmetry.

Procedure can determine how a decision is made, but not which orientation that decision ultimately embodies.[3] When outcomes carry action-authorising force, the choice of outcome necessarily privileges one ontology's harm thresholds, authority relations, or legitimacy criteria over others. The resulting dissatisfaction is not a procedural defect; it is a structural remainder.

2 'Singularity' is used descriptively rather than metaphorically. The claim is not that institutions eliminate plurality, but that they must collapse it into a determinate outcome in order to act. This constraint follows from functional necessity rather than ideological design.

3 Procedural accounts of legitimacy often assume that fair process can substitute for substantive convergence. The present claim is narrower: procedures can dampen variance, distribute loss, and stabilise expectations, but cannot eliminate ontological asymmetry where outcomes authorise action.

This explains a recurrent empirical pattern: institutions that are widely acknowledged to have followed proper procedure still generate intense and asymmetric outrage.

5.3 Power as Mediation, Not Corruption

In liberal theory, the involvement of power in decision-making is often treated as a distortion – a contaminant that enters when ideal conditions fail. Under ontological plurality, this framing is misleading.

Power does not enter institutions because procedure breaks down. It enters because procedure is insufficient to resolve underdetermination.

When reasons fail to converge, institutions must still decide. At that point, selection is stabilised through authority, enforcement, precedent, or coercive backing. Power, in this sense, is not opposed to legitimacy; it is what allows legitimacy claims to become operative at all.[4]

This does not mean that all exercises of power are justified. It means that some exercise of power is structurally unavoidable once singular outcomes are required under plural ontology.

5.4 Why Institutional Failure Is Misdiagnosed

Because liberal frameworks often assume that disagreement is ultimately reparable through better reasons or fairer procedures, persistent contestation is frequently redescribed as:

- irrationality,
- extremism,
- misinformation,
- bad faith,
- or democratic decay.

The singularity constraint offers a different diagnosis. Persistent outrage does not indicate that institutions have failed to do their job. It indicates that they have done the only job available to them: selecting one outcome where no outcome could satisfy all orientations simultaneously.

4 On power as constitutive rather than merely distortive of institutional order, see Max Weber on authority and legitimacy, and Michel Foucault on power as productive. The present argument does not endorse all exercises of power, but rejects the assumption that power enters only when institutions fail.

This reframes institutional crisis. The problem is not that institutions cannot reconcile pluralism. It is that they are repeatedly asked to do so.

5.5 Preview: Confirming Instances

The chapters that follow examine three domains where institutional singularity is especially visible:

- Science, where convergence is achieved only through engineered ontological narrowing;
- Policing, where singular decisions must be rendered under radical interpretive plurality and immediate coercive force;
- Law, where verdicts terminate dispute procedurally whilst leaving ontological conflict intact.

In each case, the same structure appears: descriptive agreement expands, procedure functions as designed, and yet evaluative disagreement persists with remarkable invariance. These are not anomalies. They are confirming instances of institutional singularity under ontological plurality.

Structural Constraint Model

THIS CHAPTER FORMALISES THE MANUSCRIPT'S CORE DEPENDENCY claims as a logical and structural model, rather than a predictive or quantitative one.[5] The purpose of the model is not to forecast outcomes, but to make explicit the relationships and constraints that render certain forms of moral, legal, and political disagreement unavoidable. Symbols are used as compressed prose to clarify dependency, underdetermination, and invariance. Readers uninterested in formal notation may skip to §6.6 without loss of argumentative continuity.

6.1 Why Formalisation Is Necessary

The argument developed in preceding chapters is frequently misread as psychological, rhetorical, or moralistic.[6] Such readings mistake descriptive claims about cognition and language for normative judgments about actors or institutions. Formalisation serves a clarifying function: it isolates which

5 The model is clarificatory rather than predictive. It does not aim to forecast outcomes, estimate probabilities, or optimise decisions, but to make explicit the dependency relations and constraints already implicit in institutional practice. Comparable uses of formalisation as conceptual clarification appear in philosophy of science and jurisprudence, where models are used to expose structure rather than generate predictions.

6 The formalisation is introduced to prevent a recurring category error: treating structural claims about constraint and underdetermination as evaluations of agent motivation, sincerity, or institutional virtue. The model abstracts away from moral appraisal in order to isolate what varies and what does not across institutional contexts.

features of institutional conflict are contingent, which are invariant, and which cannot be eliminated by improved information, better intentions, or procedural refinement.

The model introduced here is logical rather than mathematical in ambition. It does not seek numerical prediction, optimisation, or empirical estimation. Instead, it specifies modal constraints: what must follow if certain conditions obtain. The formalism does not replace the argument; it pins it in place.

6.2 The Intuitive Model

Begin with a familiar pattern. Multiple groups encounter the same salient event. Each group interprets that event through a distinct ontological orientation that structures salience prior to deliberation or language. Institutions, however, cannot preserve plural interpretations indefinitely. Courts must issue verdicts. Agencies must issue rulings. Scientific bodies must endorse conclusions. Policing organisations must classify actions as justified or not.

Disagreement enters at interpretation; institutions must nevertheless select; outrage persists regardless of outcome.

Plural interpretations enter; a single outcome exits. Which interpretation is instantiated is contingent. That at least one group experiences the outcome as injustice is not. The system behaves like a funnel: plural ontological inputs are collapsed into a singular institutional output, and dissatisfaction downstream is guaranteed.[7] This pattern is not accidental. It is constitutive of institutional decision-making under ontological plurality.

7 The funnel metaphor is structural rather than mechanical. It denotes the necessity of outcome singularity under institutional decision-making, not a causal mechanism or optimisation process. No claim is made about efficiency, fairness, or accuracy.

6.3 The Formal Model

We now introduce a minimal formal vocabulary to make this structure explicit. The formalism here is intentionally minimal: its purpose is not to generate new results beyond the prose, but to render dependency relations explicit and to block misreadings that treat persistence as contingent rather than necessary.

Definitions

- O_i: Ontological orientation of cohort i
- E: Salient event under evaluation
- L: Law and formal procedure (*statutes, precedents, admissibility rules*)
- C: Contingent human and environmental conditions (*judgment, affect, interactional dynamics*)
- I(E): Institutional interpretation of event E (*the effective law as instantiated*)
- J_i: Justice assessment of cohort i

Core Relationships

The institutional interpretation is an underdetermined mapping:[8]

$$I(E)=g(O_{judge},O(_{jury...n}),L,C)$$

Each cohort evaluates the realised outcome according to its own orientation:

$$J_i=f(I(E),O_i)$$

No probabilistic assumptions are required. The model asserts only dependency and constraint.

8 Underdetermination here means that multiple admissible interpretations satisfy the formal constraints simultaneously. It does not imply arbitrariness, indeterminacy of law, or absence of constraint. Law and procedure delimit the space of possible outcomes without uniquely fixing one.

6.4 What the Model Shows

Several conclusions follow directly.

First, I(E) is not '*the law applied to facts*'. It is the effective law, instantiated by particular agents, under particular conditions, within formal constraints that delimit but do not uniquely determine outcomes.

Second, contingency does not create injustice. It selects which ontology is realised. The role of contingent human judgment is not epistemic failure but structural mediation.

Third, disagreement is upstream of outcomes, not downstream. There is no single interpretation I(E) prior to instantiation, only a distribution of possible instantiations constrained by law and procedure.

It follows necessarily that:

For any institutional outcome, there exists at least one cohort for whom that outcome constitutes injustice.

This is not a sociological observation but a structural result.

6.5 Why Reducing Contingency Does Not Solve the Problem

A common objection holds that if contingency matters, then better jury selection, improved judicial training, or refined procedures could mitigate injustice. This objection concedes rather than refutes the argument.

Reducing contingency does not reduce ontological plurality.[1] It shifts power upstream.

When attorneys profile jurors, when venues are selected strategically, when decision-makers are filtered for reliability, what improves is not justice but predictability of selection. Ontological asymmetry remains invariant; only its management improves.

A system whose outcomes can be reliably steered is not closer to justice. It is closer to stable domination.

The ferocity of jury selection disputes is therefore diagnostic. If outcomes were determined by facts alone, juror ontology would not matter. If outcomes were determined by law alone, judicial assignment would

1 Efforts to reduce contingency – through selection mechanisms, training, or procedural refinement – alter who decides and how reliably outcomes are produced, but do not eliminate ontological variance among affected cohorts. This distinction mirrors classic critiques of technocratic governance that conflate predictability with legitimacy.

not matter. The legal system tacitly acknowledges ontological plurality by devoting immense resources to controlling who decides, not merely what is decided.

6.6 What This Clarification Does – and Does Not – Claim

This model does not imply that law is meaningless, that outcomes are arbitrary, or that institutions are dispensable. Law constrains. Procedure damps variance. Institutions stabilise expectations and enable coordination under disagreement.

What the model rules out is a comforting fiction: that justice is a determinate property waiting to be extracted once enough facts are known and enough rules are followed.

Institutions offer settlement, not reconciliation. Stability, not convergence. Maintenance, not resolution.

Once this is admitted openly, much performative outrage and metaphysical overreach can be retired.

Logical Status of the Model (Clarificatory Note)

The argument advanced here is conditional. If ontological plurality exists; if salience is assigned prior to language; if certain moral and legal terms are structurally contestable; and if institutions must issue singular outcomes; then persistent disagreement is not an anomaly but a necessity. Rejecting the conclusion therefore requires rejecting at least one of these premises. Appeals to better intentions, clearer language, or improved deliberation are insufficient.

> ***Summary for Non-Technical Readers (§6.6 Recap)***
>
> - Disagreement persists because ontologies differ, not because people are ignorant.
> - Institutions must choose one outcome even when no shared standard exists.
> - Power selects among underdetermined options.
> - Outrage is therefore predictable and unavoidable.
> - Better process reduces chaos, not conflict.

7

Power as Mediation

Hard, Soft, and Structural Stabilisation Under Ontological Plurality

The preceding chapter established a constraint: where ontological plurality meets structurally contestable terms, institutional outcomes are underdetermined by law, facts, or semantics alone. Yet institutions persist. Decisions are made, policies enforced, verdicts rendered, and coordination continues. This chapter addresses the mechanism that makes this possible. Where semantic reconciliation is structurally unavailable, power mediates.

Power is not introduced here as a moral indictment or a sociological afterthought, but as an operational necessity.[1] Institutions cannot suspend action until ontological convergence is achieved, because such convergence is often unavailable in principle. Power stabilises meaning sufficiently for coordination to continue when language cannot.

1 Power is treated here functionally rather than normatively. The claim is not that power is justified, benevolent, or immune to abuse, but that some mechanism of enforcement or stabilisation is structurally required wherever institutions must act under semantic underdetermination. This usage is closer to functional accounts in institutional theory than to moral or genealogical critiques of domination.

7.1 Power as a Functional, Not Pathological, Mechanism

Public discourse frequently treats power as a deviation from legitimacy: something that intrudes when reason fails or corruption intervenes. This framing presumes that legitimate outcomes are those secured through shared reasons, whilst power represents a breakdown of rational order. The analysis developed in this manuscript reverses that presumption.

If ontological plurality is real; if salience is assigned prior to deliberation; and if certain evaluative terms remain contestable even under shared facts; then power is not a failure mode of institutional reasoning. It is the mechanism by which institutions act at all under these conditions.[2]

Power does not resolve disagreement. It selects among underdetermined options and enforces that selection long enough for coordination to persist.

7.2 Three Forms of Power

Power operates through multiple modalities, which can be analytically distinguished even though they often interact in practice.[3]

7.2.1 Hard Power: Coercive Settlement

Hard power refers to the overt, coercive capacity to impose outcomes in acute situations. Courts issue binding judgments. Police enforce compliance. States apply sanctions. These interventions do not persuade dissenting cohorts that the outcome is just; they terminate dispute by force or threat thereof.

Hard power dominates where immediate action is required and semantic contestation cannot be tolerated. Its function is not moral persuasion but temporal closure.

---

2 The claim is not that power substitutes for reasoning, but that it resolves indeterminacy where reasons fail to uniquely determine outcomes. Reasoning constrains the space of admissible options; power selects among them when selection is required. This distinction mirrors the earlier separation between constraint and resolution.

3 The tripartite distinction between hard, soft, and structural power is analytic rather than historical or evaluative. It does not imply a developmental sequence, moral hierarchy, or exclusive categorisation. Many institutional decisions involve all three modalities simultaneously.

7.2.2 Soft Power: Norm-Setting and Agenda Control

Soft power operates by shaping what counts as reasonable, relevant, or legitimate within institutional discourse. Professional norms, expert authority, media framing, and procedural conventions determine which interpretations are taken seriously and which are marginalised.

Unlike hard power, soft power does not compel compliance directly. It conditions the interpretive environment such that certain ontologies appear natural, neutral, or inevitable, whilst others are rendered deviant or unintelligible. Soft power stabilises meaning by narrowing the range of admissible interpretations without formally excluding them.

7.2.3 Structural Power: Path Dependence and Institutional Inertia

Structural power operates over longer time horizons. It is embedded in institutional design, historical precedent, training regimes, and selection mechanisms. Once an institution stabilises around a particular ontological orientation, subsequent decisions tend to reproduce that orientation even without explicit coercion or norm enforcement.

Structural power explains why institutions exhibit inertia, why reform efforts encounter resistance even when well-intentioned, and why outcomes cluster geographically, demographically, or administratively.

This form of power is least visible and most durable. It does not decide individual cases so much as shape the space of possible decisions.

7.3 Indexing Power to Semantic Failure

The central claim of this chapter is indexed, not global.[4] Power does not dominate everywhere. It dominates where language cannot settle *Contestables* under plural orientation.

In domains governed by *Invariants* or tightly constrained observables, semantic coordination is often sufficient. Where material coupling, replication, or engineering constraint discipline interpretation, power recedes into the background.

---

4 Power is foregrounded only under specific conditions: persistent ontological plurality combined with action-authorising terms that lack shared semantic anchoring. In domains governed by invariant observables or tightly constrained procedures, semantic coordination remains sufficient and power recedes from view. No general claim is made about the primacy of power across all social interaction.

Where evaluative terms such as justice, threat, reasonable force, legitimacy, or harm remain untethered, power necessarily moves to the foreground. This is not because actors abandon reason, but because reason alone cannot determine outcomes under these conditions. Power fills the gap left by semantic underdetermination.

7.4 Power and the Illusion of Neutrality

Institutional power often presents itself as neutral, objective, or procedural. This is not merely rhetorical deception. Neutrality is a functional aspiration: institutions must appear stable and predictable to maintain legitimacy. However, neutrality does not eliminate ontological selection. It masks it.

By treating contested judgments as applications of rule rather than instantiations of orientation, institutions reduce visible conflict whilst preserving coordination. The appearance of neutrality is therefore a stabilising strategy, not an epistemic guarantee.

7.5 From Mediation to Case Studies

This framework prepares the ground for the chapters that follow.

In science, convergence is achieved by reducing ontological variance through selection, training, and material constraint, with power operating softly and structurally to enforce methodological homogeneity.

In policing, ontological homogeneity is produced through acculturation, reinforced by structural privilege, and defended through both soft and hard power when contested.

These are not anomalies. They are confirming instances of the same mechanism: where language cannot reconcile plural orientations, power stabilises meaning sufficiently for institutions to function.

The next chapters examine these cases in detail.

Science as Confirming Instance

SCIENTIFIC CONVERGENCE IS OFTEN PRESENTED AS THE STANDING objection to any thesis that emphasises semantic instability, ontological plurality, and power-mediated settlement. If '*we can't agree because our ontologies diverge*', the critic replies, '*then why can physics agree?*' The objection is rhetorically effective because it trades on a familiar myth: that science converges because it has transcended the contingencies of human orientation through method, evidence, and procedural neutrality.

This chapter argues something slightly less comforting and considerably more accurate. Scientific convergence is not a counterexample to ontological plurality. It is a confirming instance under special conditions.[1] Where convergence occurs, it is purchased through (i) the engineering of local ontological homogeneity via selection, training, and institutional filtering, and (ii) material coupling that disciplines interpretation through external constraint (replication, predictive success, technological functionality). These conditions do not eliminate plurality. They reduce it locally and relocate it elsewhere.

The payoff is twofold. First, this reframes scientific consensus as conditional, not metaphysically privileged. Second, it dissolves the naïve inference

1 The claim is not that scientific results are arbitrary or merely rhetorical, but that convergence is achieved under specific institutional and material constraints. This account is compatible with scientific realism about local results whilst rejecting the inference that convergence reflects unmediated ontological transparency.

that moral and political institutions could achieve scientific-style convergence merely by importing scientific rhetoric (*'follow the evidence'*) or method fetish (*'be rational'*). Those domains lack the very conditions that make scientific convergence possible. Expecting science-like consensus in politics is not optimistic. It is categorically confused.

8.1 What Must Be Explained

Any serious account must explain at least four things that ordinary 'science converges because evidence' narratives leave underspecified:

- **Local stability**: why many scientific terms and claims stabilise sufficiently for cumulative work.
- **Persistent controversies**: why some disputes remain entrenched for decades despite extensive data.
- **Paradigm discontinuities**:[2] why revolutions occur, and why rival frameworks are often mutually unintelligible in practice.
- **Institutional defensiveness**: why communities react with hostility when their stabilisation mechanisms are exposed.

A framework that cannot accommodate all four will either romanticise science (the rationalist myth) or trivialise it (the *'everything is power'* meme). The present thesis attempts neither. It treats science as a domain in which the general dynamics of ontological plurality are managed, not abolished.

8.2 Selection, Training, and the Manufacture of Ontological Homogeneity

Scientific communities do not begin from a neutral distribution of world-relations. They are formed through processes that select, acculturate, and filter participants into a relatively coherent cohort. This is not a conspiracy. It is an operational necessity for high-complexity work.[3] Without shared

2 See Thomas S. Kuhn, *The Structure of Scientific Revolutions* (1962), esp. chapters on incommensurability and normal science. The present account adopts Kuhn's descriptive insight whilst reframing paradigm stability as a case of engineered ontological homogeneity rather than epistemic rupture alone.

3 Selection and acculturation are treated here as functional features of high-complexity institutional work, not as evidence of ideological capture or bad faith. Comparable filtering mechanisms exist in engineering, medicine, and law wherever coordination under constraint is required.

standards of evidence, explanation, and legitimacy, laboratories cannot function, journals cannot adjudicate, and knowledge cannot stabilise even locally.

Three mechanisms matter.

8.2.1 Selection at entry

Scientific institutions select for a cluster of dispositions and tolerances: comfort with abstraction; willingness to subordinate personal meaning to procedural constraint; patience for delayed reward; and, crucially, acceptance of the epistemic authority of the scientific community. Even before formal training begins, self-selection and gatekeeping reduce variance in orientations.

This matters because it undercuts the implicit premise in many counterarguments: that science represents '*humanity reasoning together*'. It does not. It represents a specialised, filtered population reasoning within a specialised institutional ecology.

8.2.2 Acculturation as ontological bootcamp

Graduate training does not merely transmit techniques. It installs a way of seeing what counts as a question, what counts as evidence, what counts as a mistake, and what counts as a legitimate explanatory move.

It is here that ontological orientation becomes operationally prior: once installed, these standards fire pre-reflectively. A trained scientist does not deliberate over whether '*replication*' matters; it already matters. A trained physicist does not treat anecdote as a competitor to instrument readout; the hierarchy is pre-set. '*Objectivity*' functions less as a property of individual minds than as an institutionalised demand:[4] a norm that disciplines perception, attention, and justification.

This is precisely why scientific discourse appears to '*escape*' the instability described by LIH in some domains. It is not that language has become magically adequate. It is that the community has stabilised its linguistic practices through shared orientation and shared constraint.

---

4 This treatment aligns with sociological and historical accounts of scientific objectivity as a norm enforced through practice rather than a psychological state. See Lorraine Daston and Peter Galison, *Objectivity* (2007).

8.2.3 Institutional filtering and deviant exit

Peer review, hiring, promotion, grant funding, and prestige mechanisms are not neutral conveyors of truth. They are filters that maintain coherence by selecting for methodological and ontological fit. Heterodox work may succeed, but it almost always does so by building its own sub-institutions: new journals, new conferences, new departments, new funding streams. This is a form of institutional speciation.[5]

A predictable consequence follows: internal convergence produces external divergence. The better a discipline stabilises its standards, the more alien those standards may appear to outsiders. This is why cross-disciplinary disputes (economics versus sociology, psychology versus neuroscience, philosophy of mind versus cognitive science) routinely replicate the same failure modes seen in moral and political conflict: shared words, diminished shared reference, and escalating accusations of incompetence or bad faith.

Scientific convergence, then, is best understood as local agreement within engineered homogeneity, not universal agreement among plural ontologies.

8.3 Material Coupling: External Constraint as Disciplining Force

The second special condition is material coupling. Science is not merely a rhetorical arena. It is tethered to a world that pushes back. Instruments break, predictions fail, bridges collapse, molecules do not behave as desired. This external constraint disciplines discourse in ways moral and political discourse often cannot replicate.

Material coupling does three things.

1. Anchors *Invariants*: Measurement routines tether certain claims to shared procedures and observables, pushing them toward the 'Invariant' end of the LIH gradient.
2. Limits semantic drift: Operational definitions and experimental protocols constrain how terms may be used within a community, even when broader meanings remain fluid.

5 'Speciation' is used metaphorically to describe institutional divergence under selective pressure, not to imply biological analogy beyond functional separation and path dependence.

3. Provides a selection environment: Frameworks that support prediction and control gain institutional momentum; those that do not lose it.

This is why it is not enough to say '*science is just rhetoric*'. It is rhetoric under constraint.[6] But it is also why it is naïve to infer that constraint uniquely determines interpretation. Material coupling disciplines; it does not uniquely legislate meaning.

The world constrains the space of viable interpretations. It does not pick one for you. That selection still occurs through institutions and orientations.

8.4. Worked Mini-Case: Consciousness Research as Ontological Collision Under Constraint

Debates surrounding consciousness research provide a compact illustration of how apparent scientific disagreement tracks ontological orientation rather than mere evidential deficit. Despite shared data, overlapping methodologies, and good-faith participation, positions remain persistently divided over what counts as an explanation, a mechanism, or even a legitimate research question.

Consider three familiar approaches:[7] reductive physicalism, functionalism, and phenomenological or non-reductive accounts. All parties operate within the same empirical ecosystem: neuroimaging data, behavioural measures, lesion studies, computational models. There is no shortage of facts. Yet convergence does not occur.

From the present framework, the reason is structural. Competing orientations assign salience differently at a pre-verbal level. For reductive physicalists, causal closure and mechanistic tractability are non-negotiable. For functionalists, explanatory adequacy is indexed to behavioural and computational equivalence. For phenomenologically inclined researchers, first-person experience is not a dispensable residue but the primary explanandum. These commitments precede argument. They determine what is noticed, what is treated as noise, and what is dismissed as category error.

6 Material coupling constrains interpretation without uniquely determining it. Failed predictions, instrument breakdowns, and technological non-functionality act as selection pressures, not semantic adjudicators.

7 The characterisations here are schematic and intended to illustrate structural divergence, not to exhaustively represent any one research programme or individual position.

The resulting disputes are not over data points but over *Contestables*: explanation, reduction, emergence, sufficiency. These terms appear determinate within each local framework but lack shared ontological tethering across frameworks. As a result, arguments frequently pass through one another without contact. Each side experiences the others as either evasive or metaphysically extravagant.

Crucially, science does not resolve this plurality through semantic clarification. It resolves it, where it does, through constraint. Funding priorities, publication standards, training pipelines, and engineering success select for orientations that yield tractable models and reliable interventions. Over time, certain approaches dominate not because they have answered all ontological questions, but because they integrate more smoothly with the institutional and material demands of the field.

This selection pressure produces local convergence without global resolution. Researchers learn to speak a shared technical language, to bracket intractable questions, and to treat unresolved ontological disagreement as background noise rather than a live fault line. The apparent unity of the field is thus maintained by deferral, not settlement.

The hostile reception historically afforded to figures such as Kuhn, Feyerabend, and later Latour becomes intelligible on this view.[8] Their work did not threaten scientific results; it threatened the mythology that convergence reflects ontological transparency rather than disciplined coordination. The immune response was not against relativism per se, but against exposure of the mechanisms that make non-relativistic practice possible.

Seen this way, science is not a counterexample to the present thesis. It is its clearest confirming instance. Where ontological variance is aggressively reduced, where *Contestables* are tightly bounded by material constraint, and where institutional filtering enforces homogeneity, convergence emerges. Where these conditions weaken, pluralism resurfaces immediately.

This pattern is not a flaw. It is the price of collective inquiry under finite cognitive and institutional resources.

8 Kuhn (1962); Paul Feyerabend, *Against Method* (1975); Bruno Latour and Steve Woolgar, *Laboratory Life* (1979). The common thread is not relativism but exposure of stabilisation mechanisms that scientific communities rely on remaining implicit.

8.5 Mini-Case: IQ and the Nature–Nurture Dispute

The long-running debate over intelligence provides a compact illustration of ontological divergence under shared empirical conditions. Across behavioural genetics, psychology, and sociology, there is broad agreement on many descriptive facts: IQ scores show heritability within populations; environmental interventions can affect measured outcomes; distributions vary across groups; and predictive correlations exist at the population level. Disagreement does not persist because one side lacks the data.

What diverges are adequacy criteria – what counts as an acceptable explanation, and what follows normatively from empirical findings.

For one orientation, heritability signals causal structure. Explanatory success is tied to variance decomposition, model fit, and predictive stability. On this view, acknowledging genetic contribution is a prerequisite for intellectual honesty and policy realism. For another orientation, the same findings are interpreted through a harm-sensitive lens in which group-level inference threatens dignity, equality, and social legitimacy. Here, explanatory adequacy is constrained by downstream moral and political consequences, not merely by statistical robustness.

Both cohorts cite the same studies. Both appeal to scientific norms. Yet each experiences the other not as mistaken but as illegitimate – either evasive of facts or reckless with harm. Additional data do not resolve the dispute; they intensify it. Methodological refinements, meta-analyses, and replication efforts increase descriptive alignment whilst leaving evaluative disagreement untouched.

This is not a failure of science, nor evidence of bad faith.[9] It is a predictable outcome when shared evidence is filtered through incompatible ontological orientations regarding harm, agency, equality, and the moral status of group-level explanation. Convergence occurs only where institutional constraints narrow admissible questions or suppress downstream implications – confirming the broader claim that scientific agreement is engineered under conditions of reduced ontological variance, not naturally emergent from evidence alone.

9 The discussion of intelligence research is descriptive, not normative. No claims are made here regarding policy prescription, moral ranking of groups, or individual worth. The case is used solely to illustrate how shared empirical substrates can support divergent adequacy criteria under ontological plurality.

8.6 Why Kuhn, Feyerabend, and Latour Trigger Hostility

The defensive reception of Kuhn, Feyerabend, and Latour is often treated as a cultural skirmish between scientists and humanists. In the present frame it has a clearer explanation: these figures exposed the stabilisation machinery that scientific communities prefer to experience as invisible.

Kuhn's account of paradigms and incommensurability implies that 'progress' is not simply cumulative truth accretion but often a replacement of frameworks that cannot be straightforwardly compared within a shared language of justification.

Feyerabend's methodological pluralism undermines the myth that a single, universal 'scientific method' is the guarantor of legitimacy, suggesting instead that scientific practice is more opportunistic, historically contingent, and normatively messy than its own ideology admits.

Latour's laboratory studies and actor-network framing threaten the realist self-conception by showing how facts are stabilised through networks of instruments, institutions, and trained practitioners.

None of these claims require the conclusion that science is arbitrary. They require only the conclusion that scientific authority is constructed and maintained under constraint. For the working scientist, however, this often lands not as descriptive sociology but as existential sabotage: a threat to the legitimacy of the very apparatus by which local convergence is achieved.

In the terms of this manuscript: such critiques are interpreted as ontological intrusion. They are attacks on the cohort's stabilising orientation. Hostility is therefore less an argument than an immune response.

This is not a moral indictment of scientists. It is what any convergence-dependent institution does when its coherence mechanisms are exposed. The important point is structural: science does not escape power/knowledge dynamics by transcending them; it manages them through institutionalised constraint and filtering.

8.7 Paradigm Shifts as Ontological Replacement

Paradigm shifts are the clearest evidence that scientific disagreement is not always resolvable through 'more data' in the way popular science rhetoric implies.

They reveal two crucial features of scientific practice:

- Interpretation is framework-dependent: what counts as an anomaly, a measurement error, or a decisive result depends on background commitments.
- Resolution is partly institutional: shifts occur through education, hiring, journal control, and generational turnover as much as through decisive experiments.

This is not an anti-scientific claim. It is an account of why science can be both extraordinarily effective and periodically discontinuous. A scientific community may be rational within a paradigm, yet unable to adjudicate between paradigms without invoking standards that are themselves paradigm-indexed.

On the LIH frame, paradigms are precisely the mechanisms by which communities tether terms that would otherwise drift. Paradigm stability is a form of semantic and methodological scaffolding. When the scaffolding fails, the community must either repair it or replace it. Replacement is not achieved by semantics alone. It is achieved by power-mediated institutional reconfiguration under material constraint.

8.8 Persistent Scientific Controversies and the Replication Crisis

If science were simply '*evidence drives convergence*', certain disputes would not persist. Yet they do. The persistence is instructive because it shows where material coupling is insufficient to collapse interpretive plurality.

Consider domains where:

- variables are difficult to operationalise,
- measurement is indirect,
- phenomena are context-sensitive,
- and the same vocabulary carries different inferential loads across subfields.

Consciousness research, intelligence research, complex disease aetiology, behavioural interventions, and many areas of psychology and medicine all exhibit durable controversies that are not explained by ignorance alone.

These are not fringe failures. They are exactly the domains where:

- terms become *Contestable* or *Fluid*,
- experimental constraint is weaker,
- and institutional incentives (publication, novelty, career survival) amplify variance.

The replication crisis is not merely a scandal about *p-hacking* or publication bias, though those are real contributors.[10] It is also a demonstration of the thesis's core mechanism: that standards of success, interpretation, and adequacy are often indexical to sub-community orientation, even within nominally shared methodology. Researchers may agree on the formal language of replication whilst disagreeing about what counts as a faithful operationalisation, an acceptable effect size, or a meaningful null.

In short: even inside science, beyond a certain complexity threshold, more data does not guarantee convergence. It increases the burden placed on *Contestables* ('relevant effect', 'real phenomenon', 'robust finding') whose tethering depends on shared practice and institutional consensus rather than on semantics alone.

8.9 Interdisciplinarity as a Controlled Ontological Collision

Interdisciplinary work is routinely celebrated as a virtue, and it can be. But it is also a natural experiment in ontological plurality. When disciplines with different explanatory norms and legitimacy criteria are forced into contact, familiar failure modes appear:

- shared lexicon, divergent semantics
- conflicting standards of evidence
- different tolerances for ambiguity and causal complexity
- mutual accusations of naïveté or reductionism.=

This is not a moral failing of scientists. It is what happens when competing local homogeneities collide. The very mechanisms that enable convergence within a discipline produce divergence across disciplines. Interdisciplinarity

10 This claim does not deny the role of questionable research practices or incentive misalignment, but situates them within a broader structural account of semantic underdetermination and indexical adequacy criteria.

is therefore hard for structural reasons, not merely cultural ones.

This matters for a common rhetorical move in public discourse: '*we need evidence-based policy*'. The phrase imports the aura of scientific convergence into domains where the conditions for convergence do not hold. Evidence does not speak. Evidence is interpreted. Interpretation is ontologically mediated. Where the object of policy is human life under plural orientation (fairness, harm, liberty, legitimacy), evidence becomes just one input into a contestable evaluative field.

8.10 Why Scientific Convergence Cannot Simply Be Exported to Politics

At this point the core conclusion should be clear. Science converges locally because it can do at least three things that plural societies cannot do without coercion:

Select: filter participants into a cohort with shared epistemic orientation
Acculturate: train practitioners into shared standards of legitimacy
Discipline via constraint: tether claims to material coupling that punishes error

Politics cannot legitimately implement the first two at societal scale without becoming authoritarian. The third is limited because moral-political disputes often involve *Contestables* whose 'evidence' is itself ontologically indexed (what counts as harm, whose freedom counts, what legitimacy requires). Even where empirical facts are shared, their normative implications are not.

Thus scientific convergence is not evidence that ontological plurality is illusory. It is evidence that local convergence requires engineered conditions. When those conditions are absent, the persistence of disagreement is not a failure of reason. It is the expected behaviour of plural world-relations under institutional singularity.

8.11 Summary: Science Confirms the Mechanism

This chapter has argued that scientific convergence:

- is real and important,
- is partly grounded in material coupling,
- but is also enabled by selection, training, and institutional filtering that reduce local ontological variance.

The hostile reception of Kuhn, Feyerabend, and Latour is best understood not as evidence of their irrelevance but as evidence of the threat posed by exposing stabilisation mechanisms to those whose legitimacy depends on them remaining backgrounded.

Science is therefore not an escape from the dynamics of ontological plurality, contestable terms, and power-mediated settlement. It is a domain in which those dynamics are managed under special constraints. If even science cannot achieve convergence without engineering homogeneity and relying on institutional authority, then expecting moral, legal, and political domains to achieve convergence through '*better dialogue*' is not merely unrealistic. It mistakes the nature of the problem.

Shared Data, Divergent Adequacy Criteria
IQ and the Nature-Nurture Dispute

Few scientific debates better illustrate ontological divergence under shared evidence than disputes over intelligence, heritability, and group differences. The empirical substrate is unusually rich and unusually uncontested. Longitudinal twin studies, adoption studies, genome-wide association data, educational outcomes, psychometric stability, and cross-national comparisons are largely shared across camps. Disagreement persists not because the data are unknown, but because what counts as an adequate explanation is ontologically indexed.

At the level of observation, there is substantial convergence. IQ scores show statistical regularities. They correlate with educational attainment and certain life outcomes. estimates vary by population and environment but are non-zero. Environmental interventions can raise scores under some conditions, often transiently. These claims are widely accepted across the field.

The conflict emerges at the level of interpretation. Competing orientations assign salience differently to causation, responsibility, and moral risk. For some researchers, population-level heritability is a legitimate explanatory variable, constrained but real. For others, heritability is treated as a local statistical artefact that dissolves under socio-historical analysis. Still others accept the statistics but reject their relevance, insisting that explanatory adequacy must track intervention potential rather than variance decomposition.

These disagreements are not settled by additional data. New findings are absorbed, reweighted, or bracketed according to prior commitments about what explanations are for. The same regression coefficient can be cited as decisive evidence, dangerous misdirection, or irrelevant distraction. Terms such as intelligence, ability, fairness, merit, and opportunity function here as Contestables: they appear technical, but they authorise downstream action in education, policy, and distribution. Their meaning cannot be stabilised independently of ontological orientation.

Institutional convergence is achieved only through constraint. Ethical review boards, funding agencies, journal standards, and professional norms delimit which questions may be asked, how results must be framed, and which interpretations are permissible. This produces local homogeneity without resolving the underlying ontological disagreement. Researchers learn which claims are publishable, which are radioactive, and which must be accompanied by ritual disclaimers. The system coordinates activity, not belief.

Importantly, this is not a pathology of science. It is how science remains operable in domains where Contestables are unavoidable and stakes are high. Where material coupling is strong – engineering, pharmacology, instrumentation – ontological variance is aggressively filtered. Where coupling is weaker and moral loading is higher, plurality reasserts itself immediately.

The persistence of the nature–nurture dispute is therefore not an embarrassment to scientific rationality. It is a confirming instance of the present thesis: shared facts do not guarantee convergence when adequacy criteria diverge upstream. What stabilises practice is not semantic resolution, but institutional selection and constraint.

Policing as Confirming Instance

If science demonstrates how convergence can be achieved under engineered conditions of ontological homogeneity and material constraint, policing demonstrates the same mechanism operating in a domain where convergence is experienced as legitimacy by one cohort and experienced as injustice by another. The parallel is not rhetorical. It is structural.

Policing, like science, is a professional practice embedded in institutions that must act under uncertainty, risk, and time pressure. It therefore exhibits the same three features identified in the previous chapter: (i) selection and acculturation that reduce local ontological variance, (ii) institutional mechanisms that privilege certain interpretations over others, and (iii) the stabilisation of outcomes through authoritative decision rather than semantic reconciliation. Where it differs is not in structure but in stakes: the decisions are coercive, often violent, and immediately experienced by those outside the institution.

This makes policing a particularly clarifying case. The same mechanisms that are tolerated or even celebrated in science become morally intolerable to many observers when the consequences involve bodily harm or death. The analytical task is therefore not to defend or indict policing as such, but to explain why the same patterns of persistent disagreement recur despite reforms, data accumulation, and procedural refinement.[1]

1 The analysis is structural rather than prescriptive. It does not aim to justify police authority or deny abuses, but to explain why legitimacy disputes persist even under increased evidence, procedural reform, and good-faith engagement.

9.1 Selection and Acculturation as Ontological Engineering

Policing does not recruit from a neutral population.[2] It selects for particular dispositions: heightened threat sensitivity, willingness to exercise authority, tolerance for ambiguity under pressure, and readiness to act decisively in uncertain environments. Psychological screening, background checks, and training academies all function to reduce variance in how recruits perceive danger, legitimacy, and responsibility.[3]

This is not accidental.[4] Policing is a profession in which hesitation can be fatal, both to officers and to civilians. As with scientific practice, the institution cannot function if every encounter becomes an ontological debate. Shared orientation is therefore a functional requirement.

Training reinforces this orientation. Officers are taught to read situations through a threat-first lens, to prioritise command presence, and to treat non-compliance as a potential escalation vector.[5] Over time, this produces a cohort whose members share not merely rules but salience structures: what stands out, what matters, what counts as risk, and what counts as acceptable force.

---

2 Classic ethnographic and sociological studies document the acculturative effects of police training and early career socialisation on perception, salience, and judgment. See Van Maanen (1973), 'Observations on the Making of Policemen'; Skolnick (2011 [1966]), *Justice Without Trial*; and Chan (1996) on police culture as a structuring cognitive environment rather than a mere set of attitudes.

3 Empirical work on police recruitment and screening consistently shows selection effects favouring heightened threat sensitivity, authority acceptance, and tolerance for coercive action under uncertainty. See Cochrane, Tett, and Vandecreek (2003) on psychological screening in law enforcement; Scrivner (1994) on pre-employment selection criteria; and White, Cooper, Saunders, and Raganella (2010) on recruitment filtering effects. These mechanisms do not produce uniform behaviour, but they reliably reduce variance in threat perception and legitimacy judgments at entry.

4 'Not accidental' here means functionally selected and reinforced through training incentives and role demands, not intentionally orchestrated. Comparable selection/acculturation dynamics exist in any institution that must act under risk, time pressure, and uncertainty.

5 Experimental and field studies indicate that training and occupational context modulate threat perception under time pressure. See Correll et al. (2007) on shooter bias and decision thresholds; Fridell et al. (2009) on perceptual training effects; and Nieuwenhuys, Savelsbergh, and Oudejans (2012) on stress-induced attentional narrowing in police decision-making.

The result is local ontological homogeneity. Officers may disagree about tactics or judgment calls, but they largely agree – pre-verbally – about what kind of situation they are in. This mirrors scientific acculturation precisely: shared orientation enables coordinated action, but it also narrows interpretive space.

9.2 The Officer/Civilian Binary and Epistemic Asymmetry

A further structural feature distinguishes policing from many other institutions: the Officer/Civilian binary.[6] This is not merely a legal distinction. It is an ontological one that structures epistemic authority in advance of any particular encounter.

Officers are institutionally positioned as legitimate agents of force, trained observers of threat, and authorised interpreters of compliance. Civilians are positioned as potential sources of risk, objects of command, and subjects whose accounts are secondary to official interpretation. This asymmetry is codified in law, reinforced in training, and operationalised in practice.

The consequence is epistemic privilege.[7] Officer testimony is presumptively credible because it is embedded in an institutional narrative of professional judgment under danger. Civilian testimony is treated as partial, emotional, or self-interested, particularly when it conflicts with officer accounts. This is not necessarily because officers lie and civilians tell the truth, or vice versa. It is because the institution must stabilise meaning somewhere, and it stabilises it within its own ontology.

6 Legal and sociological analyses document a persistent asymmetry in epistemic credibility between officers and civilians. Officer testimony is routinely granted presumptive legitimacy grounded in institutional role and perceived professional judgment. See Slobogin (2002) on judicial deference to police narratives; Harris (2010) on credibility asymmetries in Fourth Amendment jurisprudence; and Skolnick (2011) on the 'working personality' as an epistemic filter rather than merely a behavioural one.

7 On perceived legitimacy and deference to institutional authority under conditions of asymmetry, see Tom R. Tyler, *Why People Obey the Law* (2006). The present claim concerns structural credibility assignment, not the truthfulness of any specific cohort's testimony.

This binary functions exactly like a Derridean hierarchical opposition: Officer/Civilian, Authority/Subject, Legitimate/Illegitimate.[8] The privileged term structures interpretation in advance. Attempts to evaluate encounters '*neutrally*' without acknowledging this asymmetry consistently fail because neutrality itself is ontologically indexed.

9.3 Body Cameras and the Effectiveness Horizon

Body-worn cameras are often introduced as a technological solution to moral and political disagreement.[9] The expectation is straightforward: if disputes persist because of conflicting testimony or bad faith, then objective footage should dissolve controversy.

The empirical record does not support this expectation.[10] Body-camera footage reliably increases access to *Invariants*: who moved where, when force was applied, how long an encounter lasted. It does not stabilise *Contestables*: whether the officer reasonably perceived a threat, whether force was proportionate, whether compliance was feasible, or whether authority was legitimately exercised.

This outcome is not a failure of the technology. It is a demonstration of the LIH effectiveness horizon. The camera records behaviour, not meaning. Interpretation of what is seen remains ontologically mediated.[11]

---

8 The reference is to Derrida's analysis of hierarchical oppositions as structuring meaning asymmetrically, where the privileged term governs interpretation in advance. The present claim is structural: the institutional role distinction functions as an interpretive hierarchy irrespective of individual intent.

9 Systematic reviews of body-worn camera programs consistently find increased factual agreement without corresponding convergence on evaluative judgments such as reasonableness or proportionality. See Ariel et al. (2016); Lum et al. (2019); and Braga, Sousa, Coldren, and Rodriguez (2018). These studies show reductions in some forms of dispute and misconduct reporting, but no reliable elimination of interpretive disagreement regarding justified force.

10 Empirical findings on body-worn cameras are mixed and often show increased agreement on observable sequences without resolving disagreement on evaluative judgments (e.g., reasonableness, proportionality, threat perception). The claim here is not that cameras are useless, but that they expand Invariants without tethering *Contestables*.

11 On the persistence of divergent interpretations under shared visual evidence, see Taylor (2016) on police video interpretation, and Sandhu and Hine (2017) on body-camera footage and narrative reconstruction. These findings align with broader work on visual evidence and motivated interpretation (e.g., Kahan et al. 2016).

Different cohorts routinely watch the same footage and reach incompatible conclusions, even whilst agreeing on the physical facts. For officers and their institutional allies, the footage often confirms training-consistent threat narratives. For critics, the same footage confirms excessive force or unjustified escalation. More data does not converge judgment; it relocates the disagreement.

This mirrors precisely the role of replication in science: increased data availability constrains some interpretations whilst leaving others underdetermined. In policing, the underdetermined space is precisely where moral evaluation occurs.

9.4 Why Reform Targets Miss the Mark (Without Being Useless)

Policing reform proposals overwhelmingly target downstream variables: training protocols, use-of-force policies, reporting requirements, disciplinary procedures, and technological oversight. These interventions can matter. They can reduce variance, eliminate egregious abuses, and improve accountability at the margins.[12] What they cannot do is reconcile ontological divergence.[13]

Training reforms often intensify the very orientations they seek to moderate, because they must still prepare officers to act under uncertainty. Policy refinements generate more detailed rules, which shift rather than eliminate discretion. Oversight mechanisms introduce additional institutional layers, each with its own ontological commitments. Body cameras add information without settling interpretation.

This is not because reformers are naïve or malicious. It is because they implicitly treat the problem as epistemic or procedural: if only officers were better trained, if only policies were clearer, if only evidence were available,

12 Evaluations of policing reform repeatedly show marginal improvements in specific outcomes without resolving underlying legitimacy disputes. See President's Task Force on 21st Century Policing (2015); Braga and Weisburd (2019) on evidence-based policing limits; and Nagin (2013) on deterrence, discretion, and residual conflict. These reforms modify practice without dissolving upstream divergence in threat perception and legitimacy attribution.

13 This does not imply reforms are futile. Reforms can reduce variance, constrain discretion, and increase accountability. The claim is only that procedural or informational interventions cannot guarantee evaluative convergence where disagreement is upstream in salience assignment and legitimacy criteria.

then convergence would follow. The policing case shows why this expectation is misplaced.

The core disagreement is not about what happened. It is about what counts as threat, legitimacy, and justified force. Those are *Contestables* whose evaluation is structured upstream by ontological orientation. Reform that does not address this will improve practice without dissolving outrage.

9.5 Predictable Patterns of Outrage

The formal model introduced earlier predicts the following pattern, which policing repeatedly exhibits:

1. A salient encounter occurs.
2. Institutions investigate and produce a single outcome.
3. One cohort experiences vindication; another experiences injustice.
4. Outrage persists regardless of outcome direction.
5. The cycle repeats with the next case.

Crucially, changes in outcome distribution do not eliminate the pattern. Convictions, acquittals, settlements, policy changes – each produces outrage from different quarters.[14] This is not evidence that '*no outcome will ever satisfy anyone*'. It is evidence that plural ontological orientations are being forced through a singular decision point. The outrage is signal, not noise.

14 Public response to controversial policing outcomes exhibits stable polarisation patterns independent of outcome direction. For empirical documentation, see Pew Research Center (2016, 2020) on policing legitimacy; Tyler, Jackson, and Mentovich (2015) on procedural justice divergence; and Desmond, Papachristos, and Kirk (2016) on community response following police violence.

9.6 Structural Isomorphism with Science

At this point the isomorphism with the science case should be unmistakable:[15]

- **Selection and training** produce local homogeneity.
- **Institutional authority** stabilises interpretation.
- **External inputs** (data, footage) constrain but do not determine meaning.
- **Critique of stabilisation mechanisms** triggers defensiveness.
- **Persistent disagreement** appears where Contestables dominate.

The difference is not structure but moral valence. When scientific authority stabilises meaning, the costs are often abstract or delayed. When policing authority stabilises meaning, the costs are immediate, embodied, and unequally distributed. This intensifies moral reaction but does not alter the underlying dynamics.

9.7 Maintenance, Not Resolution

Recognising policing as a confirming instance does not entail resignation. It clarifies what kinds of interventions are possible and what kinds are illusory.

What is structurally unavailable is reconciliation through better explanation. What remains available is maintenance: variance damping, damage limitation, accountability design, and institutional humility about what can and cannot be achieved.[16] This may include decentralisation, clearer jurisdictional boundaries, independent review structures, and limits on scope of authority. None of these resolve ontological divergence. They manage its consequences.

---

15 For comparative analyses of professional homogeneity, authority, and interpretive closure, see Collins and Evans (2007) on expertise and boundary work; Bourdieu (1988) on field reproduction; and Longino (1990) on constrained pluralism in epistemic communities. The present claim concerns structural similarity, not moral equivalence.

16 On institutional maintenance under persistent disagreement, see Hirschman (1970) on exit, voice, and loyalty; Ostrom (1990) on governance without consensus; and Mouffe (2005) on agonistic pluralism. The contribution here is not normative endorsement but structural diagnosis.

The central lesson is the same as in science: convergence is not a natural resting state achieved by adding information or refining language. It is an engineered outcome achieved under specific conditions. Where those conditions cannot be ethically or practically imposed, persistent disagreement is not a failure to be solved but a reality to be designed around.

9.8 Summary

Policing confirms the thesis under harsher lighting. It shows that:

- ontological homogeneity is produced, not discovered;
- epistemic asymmetry is structurally embedded;
- technological transparency expands Invariants without tethering Contestables;
- reform efforts that ignore upstream divergence will disappoint without being meaningless.

Most importantly, it shows why outrage persists even when institutions 'work as intended'. The problem is not that the system fails to deliver justice in some absolute sense. It is that justice itself is a *Contestable* evaluated through incompatible orientations, and institutions cannot instantiate more than one at a time.

The policing case therefore does not stand apart from the scientific one. Together, they demonstrate that where language reaches its effectiveness horizon, institutions stabilise meaning through authority. The question is not how to eliminate this fact, but how to live with it without pretending it is something else.

Interlude: *Police Discretion and Jury Adjudication as Temporal Variants*

Policing and jury adjudication are often treated as categorically distinct sites of moral and legal judgment: the former discretionary and contingent, the latter deliberative and rule-bound. From the perspective developed here, this contrast is overstated. Both operate as mechanisms for collapsing ontological plurality into singular outcomes. What differs is not kind, but temporal structure.[17]

17 The claim is not that policing and jury adjudication are morally or legally identical, but that they perform the same structural function – collapsing ontological plurality into singular outcomes – under different temporal conditions. The distinction is analytic rather than normative.

Police discretion is ontological selection under time pressure.[18] Officers must act in compressed temporal windows, under uncertainty, and with limited access to justificatory resources. Salience assignment, threat perception, and legitimacy judgments are therefore foregrounded, whilst narrative reconstruction occurs later, if at all. The outcome is immediate, embodied, and often irreversible.

Jury adjudication performs the same selection function under extended temporal conditions. Evidence is filtered, narrated, sequenced, and formally constrained. *Contestables* are translated into jury instructions, legal standards, and verdict forms. The process gives the appearance of semantic control and rational convergence, but the underlying mechanism remains unchanged:[19] a group of situated agents, each carrying ontological orientations, must render a singular judgment over untethered action-terms such as intent, reasonableness, proportionality, and justification.

In both cases, institutions do not resolve ontological conflict. They defer, compress, or ritualise it.

This temporal distinction explains a recurring pattern in public reaction. Police actions are contested immediately and viscerally, whilst jury verdicts are contested symbolically and retrospectively. Yet the structure of outrage is identical. In both cases, one orientation is instantiated and others are negated. What differs is the latency of recognition and the vocabulary available for protest.

The frequent appeal to jury trials as a corrective to police discretion therefore misfires. Trials do not eliminate ontological asymmetry; they redistribute it across time, procedure, and personnel. The officer's salience judgment is replaced by the jury's collective salience judgment, mediated by law and rhetoric but not ontologically neutralised.

This is why acquittals following controversial police encounters are often experienced not as closure but as confirmation of injustice. The legal process has functioned correctly, yet the losing cohort experiences

18 'Ontological selection' here refers to the operation of pre-reflective salience under constraint, not to conscious choice or moral reasoning. The claim concerns structural conditions of action, not the motivations or character of individual officers.

19 Extended deliberation increases procedural formality and justificatory density, but does not eliminate ontological variance among decision-makers. Jury adjudication redistributes ontological selection across time, narrative, and institutional ritual rather than neutralising it.

the verdict as a second injury rather than a resolution.[20] The problem is not insufficient deliberation. It is that deliberation has been asked to do work it cannot perform.

Seen this way, policing and adjudication form a continuous institutional spectrum rather than opposing poles. One selects quickly under constraint; the other selects slowly under ceremony. Both are singularity machines operating on contestable moral terrain.

This continuity sets the stage for the legal verdict case study that follows, where the full architecture of ontological selection, procedural dampening, and asymmetric outrage can be observed in its most explicit and socially legible form.

Interpretive Note for Isomorphic Table for Science and Policing Claims

This table does not claim that science and policing are morally equivalent, normatively comparable, or politically interchangeable. The claim is strictly structural.[21]

Both domains achieve local stability by:

- reducing ontological variance through selection and training,
- expanding access to Invariants through instrumentation,
- leaving high-salience Contestables structurally underdetermined,
- and relying on institutional authority to collapse plurality into singular outcomes.

Where science enjoys strong material coupling, convergence is sustained. Where policing lacks such coupling, contestation persists. The difference is not moral sophistication but constraint density.

20 'Second injury' is used descriptively to denote the reactivation or confirmation of perceived injustice through institutional closure, not as a clinical or psychological diagnosis.

21 Structural isomorphism does not imply moral equivalence, political symmetry, or evaluative parity. It denotes similarity in functional architecture under constraint, not similarity in ethical stakes or social consequences.

Table 2: Science and Policing Claims Isomorphic

Dimension	Science	Policing
Ontological Orientation (Local)	Trained scientific realism constrained by disciplinary norms, modelling assumptions, and evidentiary practices	Trained authority-centred orientation prioritising threat detection, compliance, and control
Selection & Acculturation	Long training pipelines, peer filtering, credentialing, methodological socialisation	Recruitment screening, academy training, field acculturation, informal norm transmission
Operational Priority (Pre-verbal)	Pattern recognition, anomaly detection, signal vs noise discrimination	Threat assessment, dominance cues, compliance signals
Epistemic Asymmetry	Expert / non-expert divide; access to methods, models, and tacit knowledge	Officer / civilian divide; asymmetry in authority, risk exposure, and situational control
Institutional Goal	Produce convergent explanations sufficient for prediction, control, and engineering	Produce immediate order, compliance, and risk minimisation in dynamic environments
Role of Language	Formalised reporting, publication, and peer review narrate downstream justification	Commands, legal language, and post-hoc reports narrate downstream justification
Material Coupling	Strong: replication, prediction, technological constraint, engineering failure	Weak–moderate: physical force, bodily harm, legal review after the fact
Invariants (Expanded by Instrumentation)	Measurement data, experimental outcomes, replicated effects	Body-cam footage, timestamps, location data
Contestables (Remain Untethered)	Theory choice, interpretation, explanatory adequacy, significance	Threat perception, reasonable force, intent, compliance

Dimension	Science	Policing
Response to Disagreement	Closure through consensus, marginalisation, or paradigm boundary-setting	Closure through arrest, force, or post-hoc legal adjudication
Perception of Legitimacy	High within the trained community; opaque externally	High within policing institutions; contested externally
Failure Mode	Paradigm conflict mistaken for irrationality or ideology	Moral outrage mistaken for procedural failure or bad faith
Public Misreading	'Science reveals objective truth'	'The law was (or wasn't) applied correctly'
Structural Reality	Convergence is engineered under constraint, not discovered	Settlement is enforced under constraint, not reconciled

Rational Convergence and Its Discontents: Rawls, Habermas, and the Liberal Repair Fantasy

MUCH OF MODERN POLITICAL PHILOSOPHY IS ANIMATED BY A shared hope: that persistent moral disagreement can, in principle, be resolved through the right kind of reasoning under the right conditions. Whether framed in terms of fairness, reciprocity, or communicative rationality, this tradition assumes that conflict is ultimately epistemic or procedural rather than ontological. If agents reason sincerely, bracket parochial interests, and appeal to shared standards, convergence should follow. This manuscript rejects that hope – not as naïve, but as mislocated.[22]

10.1 Rawls: Convergence by Abstraction

Rawls' project is exemplary. By asking agents to reason behind a *veil of ignorance*, Rawls seeks to strip away contingent identities and surface shared rational commitments. Justice, on this view, is what remains once irrelevant differences are excluded and fair procedure is applied.

22 The rejection concerns the scope of the convergence claim, not the value of rational deliberation as such. The argument is that rational procedures presuppose conditions of ontological alignment that cannot be guaranteed under pluralism, not that such procedures are incoherent or worthless.

The difficulty is not that Rawls fails to anticipate pluralism. On the contrary, Political Liberalism explicitly acknowledges '*reasonable pluralism*' as a permanent feature of modern societies. The difficulty is that Rawls treats pluralism as manageable through abstraction.

From the present perspective, this move fails for a structural reason. The veil of ignorance presumes that ontological orientation is detachable from reasoning.[23] It assumes that salience assignment, threat perception, and legitimacy tracking can be suspended long enough for neutral principles to emerge. But if ontological orientation operates pre-verbally and pre-reflectively, then abstraction does not neutralise it; it merely conceals its operation.

Agents behind the veil do not stop being authority-sensitive, autonomy-sensitive, harm-sensitive, or order-sensitive. They carry those orientations into the abstraction itself. What appears as convergence is therefore not ontological reconciliation but orientation-consistent agreement under constrained imagination. The disagreement returns the moment abstraction is lifted and institutions must act.

Rawls offers a powerful account of fairness under shared ontological conditions. He does not offer a solution to ontological plurality.

10.1.1 Veil Leakage: A Concrete Illustration

Consider punishment proportionality in criminal sentencing. Behind the veil of ignorance, agents are asked to abstract from their social position and reason about just principles governing punishment. Yet even in this stylised setting, ontological orientation leaks immediately. An authority-weighted orientation tends to frame proportionality in terms of deterrence, order preservation, and institutional credibility: harsher punishment is justified insofar as it stabilises norms and discourages future harm. An autonomy-weighted orientation, by contrast, frames proportionality in terms of individual rights, moral desert, and error tolerance: punishment severity must be tightly constrained to minimise wrongful coercion. Both positions can accept identical facts about crime rates, recidivism, and legal procedure; the divergence arises in what counts as an acceptable risk of harm and which

23 Rawls' use of abstraction is methodologically elegant and internally coherent. The present critique does not deny this, but questions whether abstraction can suspend pre-reflective salience structures that operate prior to explicit reasoning. The issue is not fairness of procedure, but the depth at which orientation operates.

harms are morally salient. The veil does not eliminate this divergence because the evaluative weights are not downstream of social position but upstream of reasoning itself. What Rawlsian abstraction brackets is contingency of status, not ontological orientation. As a result, the original position cannot neutralise disagreements over proportionality, harm thresholds, or legitimacy; it merely postpones their institutional manifestation.

10.2 Habermas: Convergence by Communication

Habermas' wager is different but structurally similar. Where Rawls abstracts, Habermas idealises. His theory of communicative action holds that under conditions of sincerity, symmetry, and freedom from domination, rational discourse can generate legitimate norms binding on all participants. These conditions are explicitly regulative rather than empirical; the critique here concerns not their realism, but their presumed sufficiency.

Deliberative mechanisms do achieve convergence under conditions of limited ontological variance, shared role orientation, and low action-authorisation. The claim here is not that deliberation fails universally, but that its success conditions are narrower than liberal theory typically acknowledges.

Here again, the issue is not bad faith or empirical implausibility. It is ontological misplacement.

Communicative rationality presumes that participants share enough background orientation for reasons to register symmetrically. But if salience is assigned prior to language, then discourse does not discover shared commitments; it activates pre-existing ones. The very features that Habermas treats as distortions – power, affect, identity, threat – are not removable contaminants but constitutive conditions of interpretation, shaping what counts as a reason before discourse begins.[24]

As a result, discourse under plural ontology does not converge but escalates, as each attempt at clarification intensifies the salience of the very commitments under dispute. Each side experiences the other not as mistaken but as unintelligible, evasive, or morally opaque. The failure is then redescribed as irrationality, extremism, or bad faith, rather than recognised as a structural limit of language under ontological divergence.

24 The critique concerns the presumption that these factors can be bracketed without remainder for the purposes of norm generation. The claim is not that Habermas is empirically naïve, but that communicative rationality presupposes a degree of shared ontological orientation that cannot be assumed in high-stakes plural contexts.

Habermas offers an account of norm generation within relatively homogeneous lifeworlds. He does not offer a mechanism for reconciliation between incompatible ontological orientations.

10.3 The Shared Assumption: Language as Primary Mediator

What unites Rawls and Habermas is a deeper commitment: that language, properly constrained, can serve as the primary mediator of moral and political disagreement.[1] Whether through abstraction or ideal discourse, both models presuppose that reasons can do the work that power currently does.

The Language Insufficiency Hypothesis challenges this presupposition directly. At high levels of conceptual and social complexity, language does not converge meaning; it multiplies interpretations whilst preserving the appearance of shared reference. The result is not misunderstanding but overconfidence: each side believes it is arguing within a shared frame whilst in fact speaking past ontologically incompatible commitments.

From this perspective, Rawlsian and Habermasian projects are not wrong so much as under-scoped. They describe what happens when ontological variance has already been reduced. They do not explain how plural societies persist when it has not.

Enlightenment ideals of reason, rationality, and logic are not rejected by this framework, but re-situated. Reason does not operate on a neutral substrate; it operates within ontological priors that determine what is salient, what counts as evidence, and which trade-offs are admissible. Distinct ontological orientations therefore support internally coherent but mutually irreducible forms of rationality. Persistent disagreement under these conditions is not a failure of logic or good faith, but the predictable result of reasoning applied to incommensurable evaluative foundations. This explains why highly educated groups polarise, why expert panels disagree bitterly, and why transparency often intensifies rather than resolves conflict.

1 Despite methodological differences, both projects treat linguistic reason-giving as the principal mechanism for legitimating outcomes. The present framework challenges this shared assumption by arguing that language itself is constrained by upstream ontological priors.

10.4 From Resolution to Maintenance

The consequence is not despair, but reorientation. If convergence cannot be guaranteed, then political legitimacy cannot rest on the promise of eventual agreement. Institutions must instead be evaluated by their capacity to manage ontological plurality:[2] damping variance, distributing loss, containing escalation, and preventing catastrophic failure.

This is not a retreat from normativity. It is a rejection of a particular normative fantasy: that justice is something we arrive at together, rather than something we impose, contest, endure, and renegotiate under constraint.

Rawls and Habermas offer blueprints for moral harmony. This manuscript offers a diagnosis of why harmony repeatedly fails – and why insisting upon it may be making things worse.

The tragedy of liberal optimism is not that it aspires too high, but that it mistakes ontological conflict for a communicative defect – and then treats the persistence of disagreement as a moral failing rather than a structural condition.

2 'Maintenance' is not offered as a cynical substitute for justice, but as a realist criterion under conditions where reconciliation is structurally unavailable. The claim concerns institutional evaluation, not moral resignation.

11

From Diagnosis to Design: Why Maintenance Replaces Resolution

At this point, a familiar objection begins to form. If moral and political disagreement is ontological rather than epistemic, if language cannot stabilise meaning across divergent salience structures, and if institutions must nevertheless act, then what remains of justice, legitimacy, or reform? Does this diagnosis not collapse into quietism, cynicism, or a tacit endorsement of power?[1]

It does not. But it does require abandoning a category mistake that has dominated modern political theory: the assumption that persistent disagreement signals a failure of information, reasoning, or procedure, rather than a structural feature of plural social reality.

The modernist inheritance is clear. From deliberative democracy to communicative rationality, from Rawlsian public reason to contemporary '*bridging divides*' initiatives, political legitimacy is repeatedly tied to the prospect of convergence. Disagreement is tolerated provisionally, as something to be overcome through clarification, inclusion, or improved process. When convergence fails to materialise, the diagnosis defaults to pathology: misinformation, irrationality, bad faith, capture, or affective polarisation.

1 The concern is understandable but misplaced. The argument does not deny the relevance of justice, legitimacy, or reform; it relocates them within a framework that does not presuppose eventual convergence. The issue is not whether institutions should be constrained, but how constraint operates under persistent ontological plurality.

The preceding chapters have argued that this diagnosis is often mistaken. In many of the most consequential moral and political conflicts, disagreement persists not because the parties lack shared facts, values, or vocabulary, but because they operate from incompatible ontological orientations that structure salience pre-verbally. Language enters only downstream, tasked with reconciling commitments that were never jointly instantiated. Appeals to clearer definitions or better reasoning therefore reach an effectiveness horizon beyond which additional deliberation produces diminishing, and sometimes negative, returns.

The science and policing cases sharpen this point. Scientific communities achieve local convergence by aggressively reducing ontological variance through selection, training, and institutional filtering, supplemented by material coupling that disciplines interpretation. Police institutions achieve coherence through analogous mechanisms of acculturation and in-group epistemic privilege, reinforced by hierarchical binaries that structure interpretation in advance. Both cases demonstrate that convergence is not achieved by semantic transcendence, but by engineering homogeneity. Where such engineering is ethically or politically unacceptable, convergence cannot be assumed.

Democratic institutions, however, face a further constraint. Unlike scientific disciplines or closed professional orders, they cannot legitimately eliminate ontological plurality at scale. They must govern populations whose orientations diverge along multiple, non-negotiable dimensions, whilst nevertheless producing singular outcomes: verdicts, policies, allocations, and enforcement decisions. This is the institutional singularity constraint identified earlier. It is here that the demand for reconciliation becomes not merely unrealistic, but conceptually confused.

Once this constraint is acknowledged, the task facing institutions must be reformulated. The relevant question is no longer '*How do we achieve moral convergence?*' but '*How do we act, repeatedly and sustainably, under conditions where convergence is structurally unavailable?*' The answer to this question is not resolution, but maintenance.

Maintenance, as used here, is not a moral ideal and not a consolation prize.[2] It is a design objective. It names the set of strategies by which institutions contain conflict, distribute loss, dampen variance, and minimise catastrophic failure in environments of persistent ontological plurality. Maintenance does not aim to make all outcomes feel just. It aims to ensure that no outcome renders the system intolerable to those whose orientation it negates.

This reframing immediately clarifies several recurrent confusions. First, it explains why procedural refinement so often disappoints. Improving transparency, fairness, or due process can reduce outcome variance and increase tolerability, but it cannot eliminate asymmetry where incompatible ontologies collide. Better procedure does not reconcile orientations; it makes power more predictable and, in some cases, more bearable. Treating procedural failure as the cause of persistent outrage therefore misidentifies a structural condition as a fixable defect.

Second, it dissolves the charge of nihilism. To say that institutions cannot reconcile incompatible ontologies is not to deny the reality of harm, the importance of accountability, or the necessity of constraint on power. It is to insist that these goods cannot be secured through semantic convergence alone. Power does not enter politics because language failed accidentally; it enters because institutions must act where language lacks the capacity to adjudicate. The question is not whether power will operate, but how visibly, how predictably, and with what distribution of loss.[3]

Third, it shifts evaluative emphasis from correctness to sustainability. Under conditions of acknowledged plurality, legitimacy cannot rest on universal endorsement of outcomes. It must rest on the system's capacity to survive repeated asymmetric losses without escalating into breakdown. This is a different metric from justice-as-resolution, but it is not an arbitrary one. Systems that fail this test do not merely offend philosophical sensibilities; they collapse empirically.

2 'Maintenance' names a design orientation rather than a moral theory. It concerns institutional endurance, variance containment, and loss distribution under conditions where reconciliation is structurally unavailable. It does not prescribe moral indifference, but rejects the expectation that legitimacy depends on shared endorsement of outcomes.

3 Acknowledging the inevitability of power under institutional singularity does not entail endorsement of its unrestricted use. On the contrary, making power legible, constrained, and contestable is a central maintenance objective.

Recognising maintenance as the appropriate design goal also clarifies the limited but genuine role of reform. Reforms that target downstream procedures whilst leaving upstream ontological divergence intact should not be expected to resolve conflict. At best, they redistribute it across time, space, or institutional layers. This does not render such reforms pointless. It specifies their function. Appeals to '*better training*', '*clearer standards*', or '*more dialogue*' can succeed in reducing volatility or increasing predictability, even as they leave core disagreements untouched.

Finally, this reframing prepares the ground for institutional design without illusion. Once convergence is abandoned as a default expectation, a different set of levers comes into focus: spatial distribution of authority through federalism or subsidiarity; temporal distribution through sunset clauses and rotation; procedural visibility that makes power legible rather than opaque; exit options that allow plural orientations to persist without constant collision; and role separation that prevents any single ontology from dominating all stages of decision and enforcement.

These mechanisms do not resolve ontological conflict. They manage it. They do not produce harmony. They produce endurance.

A further discomfort must be acknowledged. Democracy and capitalism present themselves as neutral procedural systems, yet they encode specific ontological commitments: individualised agency, consent-based authority, tolerance for loss distribution through markets and elections, and implicit universalism regarding their own legitimacy. Support for these systems is not the neutral baseline from which deviations must be explained, but itself an ontological inheritance acquired through acculturation long before explicit instruction. Civic education and market literacy function not merely as information transfer but as ontological assimilation – a process largely invisible to those already inside it. This does not render democracy or capitalism illegitimate, but it does strip them of their claimed neutrality. Maintenance-oriented design must acknowledge this: liberal pluralism is itself a particular ontological stance, not the view from nowhere.[4]

The chapters that follow take up this task explicitly. Having diagnosed the structural source of persistent moral and political conflict, the question

4 This claim does not deny the practical or moral appeal of liberal institutions. It denies only their neutrality. Treating liberal norms as the default epistemic baseline obscures the acculturative processes by which they become taken for granted.

becomes not how to reconcile what cannot be reconciled, but how to design institutions that acknowledge this fact without collapsing into paralysis or domination. Maintenance is not a retreat from justice. It is what justice becomes once reconciliation is recognised as a category error.

12

Maintenance Over Resolution

12.1 Resolution as a Category Error

THE DOMINANT NORMATIVE ASPIRATION IN LIBERAL POLITICAL theory is resolution: convergence on shared judgments through facts, reasons, and procedures. This aspiration presupposes that disagreement is primarily epistemic or semantic and therefore tractable via improved information flow or deliberative design.

Under ontological plurality, this aspiration becomes a category error.[1]

Where action-authorising *Contestables* are untethered from shared ontological reference, no amount of semantic refinement can force convergence. Institutions that treat persistent disagreement as evidence of procedural failure misdiagnose the problem and repeatedly overcorrect, often intensifying conflict by escalating the stakes of each decision.

Maintenance begins from a more austere premise: persistent moral disagreement is not an anomaly to be eliminated but a structural feature to be managed.

---

1 The error lies in treating persistent disagreement as evidence of insufficient information or procedure, rather than as a consequence of incompatible ontological salience structures governing what counts as harm, legitimacy, or justification.

12.2 Maintenance Defined

Maintenance refers to institutional strategies that stabilise coordination under conditions of irreducible disagreement. Its objectives are deliberately modest:

- **Variance damping**: reducing outcome volatility across time and jurisdictions
- **Loss distribution**: ensuring that no single cohort absorbs cumulative losses indefinitely
- **Containment**: preventing local moral collisions from cascading into systemic breakdown
- **Survivability**: preserving institutional legitimacy despite asymmetric dissatisfaction

Maintenance does not aim at moral convergence. It aims at institutional durability in the presence of moral plurality.[2]

12.3 Design Levers for Maintenance

The following mechanisms recur across domains where plural ontologies coexist without resolution. None dissolve disagreement. All alter how disagreement is lived.[3]

12.3.1 Federalism and Jurisdictional Separation

Federalism distributes moral authority spatially, allowing incompatible orientations to instantiate locally without requiring universal endorsement.

Illustrative case:

Cannabis legalisation in the United States demonstrates this logic in practice. What would be irresolvable at a national scale becomes tolerable through state-level divergence. Conflict does not disappear, but it is de-pressurised by jurisdictional separation. The system absorbs plurality by refusing to force premature settlement.

2 Durability here does not mean moral indifference. It refers to the capacity of institutions to survive repeated asymmetric losses without cascading delegitimation or coercive escalation.

3 The illustrative cases that follow are not offered as normative endorsements but as empirical demonstrations of maintenance mechanisms in operation: spatial separation (federalism), temporal redistribution (sunset clauses), justificatory visibility, and exit. Each alters the phenomenology and distribution of moral loss without eliminating underlying disagreement.

Federalism does not solve moral disagreement. It contains it geographically.

12.3.2 Rotation, Term Limits, and Sunset Clauses

Where moral legitimacy decays under shifting threat perceptions or cultural change, temporal limits prevent any single orientation from becoming permanently entrenched.

Illustrative case:

Sunset provisions in the USA PATRIOT Act forced periodic renegotiation of surveillance authority rather than allowing a single post-crisis security ontology to ossify. Reauthorisation debates remained contentious, but the mechanism acknowledged that legitimacy is time-sensitive rather than absolute.

Rotation redistributes moral loss across time rather than across groups alone.

12.3.3 Procedural Visibility and Justification

Visibility does not produce agreement, but it alters the phenomenology of loss. When reasoning is opaque, dissatisfaction mutates into suspicion and delegitimation.

Illustrative case:

Federal sentencing guidelines requiring written judicial justifications do not eliminate disagreement over proportionality or fairness. They do, however, reduce accusations of arbitrariness by making the interpretive path legible, even to those who reject its premises.

Visibility stabilises institutions not by persuading losers, but by limiting the scope of grievance escalation.

12.3.4 Exit Options and Institutional Choice

Exit mechanisms allow agents with incompatible ontological commitments to separate without demanding universal accommodation.

Illustrative case:

School choice and charter systems permit divergent educational ontologies – standardisation versus autonomy, secular versus religious – to coexist within a single polity. Conflict over funding and oversight remains, but existential conflict over pedagogy is partially displaced. Exit is not harmony.

12.3.5 Recognition of Assimilation as Non-Neutral

Maintenance design must acknowledge that what presents as civic competence or rational participation often encodes ontological requirements. Voter eligibility schemes, civic education curricula, and professional qualification standards do not merely filter for capacity – they filter for ontological alignment, often implicitly. Disenfranchisement schemes can be read as ontological interventions: rather than resolving moral disagreement, they reduce it by excluding populations whose evaluative orientations are known to diverge. Framed as neutral procedural safeguards, such measures function as selective ontology filters – achieving convergence not through persuasion but through elimination.[4]

This does not render all qualification standards illegitimate. It requires honesty about their function. A maintenance-oriented system acknowledges that '*political competence*' and '*ontological divergence*' are not cleanly separable, and designs accordingly – minimizing exclusion where possible, making it explicit where necessary, and ensuring excluded orientations retain voice through other channels.

12.4 Why Maintenance Is Not Conservatism

Maintenance is often misread as acquiescence to existing power. This misreading stems from conflating the inevitability of power mediation with endorsement of its current distribution. Maintenance does not sanctify outcomes. It acknowledges constraints.

A system that recognises ontological plurality can still be reformist, redistributive, and responsive. What it cannot promise is moral reconciliation through discourse alone. Maintenance reframes legitimacy from '*everyone agrees*' to '*no one is permanently excluded from influence*'.

4 Descriptive acknowledgment of this function is not an endorsement of exclusionary practice. It is an argument for institutional honesty about how legitimacy is operationalised and for the design of compensatory channels of influence where exclusion cannot be avoided.

12.5 Design Failure Modes

Maintenance mechanisms fail when:

- Loss distribution becomes one-sided or permanent
- Exit options collapse into stratified segregation
- Visibility becomes performative rather than informative
- Federalism becomes abdication rather than accommodation

These are not arguments against maintenance, but reminders that maintenance itself requires maintenance.

12.6 Transition

The next chapter examines what happens when maintenance fails or is unavailable – specifically in legal verdicts, where institutions must issue singular outcomes under maximal salience, minimal exit, and high identity load. Law exposes the limits of both resolution and maintenance with unusual clarity.

13

Legal Verdicts and the Invariance of Outrage

Legal verdicts occupy a privileged place in modern moral imagination. They are widely treated as the point at which facts are settled, norms are applied, and justice is rendered. Trials are meant to be the civilised alternative to vengeance: reason displacing passion, procedure displacing power.

And yet, in precisely the cases that matter most, verdicts fail to perform this legitimating function. Outrage persists after acquittals and after convictions. Appeals to evidence, instructions, and due process do not converge judgment. Instead, they often intensify disagreement.

This chapter argues that this persistence is not accidental. It is the predictable result of ontological plurality forced through institutional singularity.

13.1 Step 0: Factual Convergence Is Not the Problem

Before turning to interpretation, it is essential to establish what is not at issue.

In many high-profile trials, opposing camps converge on core facts. They may disagree about emphasis or framing, but not about the basic sequence of events.

Consider the typical post-verdict landscape:

- The defendant fired the weapon.
- One or more people died.
- Video footage exists.
- Witness testimony was presented.
- The legal standard applied is known.

Survey data repeatedly show that large portions of opposing cohorts agree on these points.[1] Disagreement persists not because one side believes the shooting never happened or the death was staged, but because agreement on facts does not settle evaluation.

This alone is sufficient to undermine purely epistemic accounts. If disagreement were primarily about information, convergence would track clarification. It does not.

13.2 Contestables at the Centre of Legal Judgment

Legal verdicts turn not on *Invariants*, but on *Contestables* that meet every structural criterion outlined earlier. Three recur with remarkable consistency:

'Self-defence' / 'Reasonable force'

- Distance from observables: No empirical threshold defines 'reasonable'.
- Dependence on thick ethical concepts: Intent, fear, proportionality.
- Identity-load-bearing: Defender vs. aggressor is morally constitutive.
- Action-authorising: Determines criminal liability.
- Temporal/modal loading: What should have been done under uncertainty.

1 Empirical work on post-verdict opinion consistently finds substantial agreement on core event facts and procedural details even where moral disagreement remains extreme. See, e.g.,
– Kahan, D. M. et al. (2011). Cultural cognition of public policy: The case of gun control. *Law & Human Behavior.*
– Kahan, D. M. (2017). Misconceptions, misinformation, and the logic of identity-protective cognition. Cultural Cognition Project Working Paper.
– Bartels, L. M. (2002). Beyond the running tally: Partisan bias in political perceptions. *Political Behavior.*
These studies show that polarisation clusters around evaluative judgment rather than descriptive belief, particularly in cases involving lethal force or high identity load.

'Threat'

- Observable cues underdetermine threat perception.
- Evaluated through priors about danger, authority, and legitimacy.
- Functions almost entirely counterfactually: what might have happened.

'Victim' vs. 'Perpetrator'

- Role assignment precedes moral evaluation.
- Competing dyads cannot be simultaneously instantiated.
- Once assigned, downstream interpretation follows mechanically.

These terms are not vague by accident.[2] They are structurally untethered because tethering them would require ontological agreement that does not exist.

13.3 Ontological Dimensions Activated

Legal verdicts reliably activate a small cluster of ontological dimensions, though their weighting varies across cohorts:

Authority vs. Autonomy

Who may legitimately exercise force, and under what conditions?

Threat Location

Is danger situated in the armed individual, the surrounding crowd, the state, or the absence of control?

Temporal Framing

Should actions be judged as split-second decisions or as part of a longer causal chain?

Moral Baseline

Is restraint the default expectation, or is assertive self-protection?

2 For the structural indeterminacy of legal action-terms such as 'reasonable force', 'self-defence', and 'threat', see:
- Hart, H. L. A. (1961). *The Concept of Law*, ch. 7, on open-textured standards.
- Gallie, W. B. (1956). Essentially contested concepts. *Proceedings of the Aristotelian Society*.
- Solan, L. M. & Tiersma, P. M. (2005). *Speaking of Crime: The Language of Criminal Justice*.

The present claim extends these accounts by arguing that indeterminacy persists not merely because of linguistic vagueness, but because tethering would require prior ontological agreement on salience, proportionality, and acceptable risk.

Different cohorts do not merely answer these questions differently. They experience them as differently salient. This is the pre-verbal structuring at work.

13.4 Institutional Singularity and Outcome Selection

Despite this plurality, the legal system must decide. The jury must return a verdict. The court must pronounce a judgment.

Formally, the outcome is produced by:

$$I(E)=g(O_{judge},O(_{jury...n}),Law,Procedure,RNG)$$

This is not a cynical claim. It is an accurate one.[1]

- Law and procedure constrain the outcome space.
- The ontologies of participants determine how evidence and standards are interpreted.
- RNG variables – jury composition, courtroom dynamics, narrative emphasis, credibility cues – select among underdetermined branches.[2]

Importantly, reducing contingency does not eliminate asymmetry. It merely makes its distribution more predictable. Better jury selection does not remove injustice; it increases the reliability with which one ontology is instantiated.

1 Contingent variables such as jury composition, narrative sequencing, credibility perception, and courtroom dynamics do not negate legal constraint; they select among outcomes already underdetermined by shared law and fact. Recognising this does not impugn verdicts. It describes how singular decisions are produced under plurality.

2 On the contingent but non-arbitrary role of jury composition, narrative framing, and credibility assessment in verdict formation, see:
- Pennington, N. & Hastie, R. (1992). Explaining the evidence: Tests of the story model for juror decision making. *Journal of Personality and Social Psychology*.
- Diamond, S. S. & Rose, M. R. (2005). Real juries. *Annual Review of Law and Social Science*.
- Devine, D. J. et al. (2001). Jury decision making: 45 years of empirical research. *Psychology, Public Policy, and Law*.
These factors do not override legal constraint; they select among outcomes already underdetermined by shared law and fact.

13.5 Justice Evaluation Is Deterministic Given Ontology

Once an outcome is produced, cohort reactions follow deterministically:

$$J_i=f(O_i,I(E))$$

This explains the empirical regularity that puzzles commentators: outrage is invariant with respect to outcome.[3]

- An acquittal vindicates one ontology and negates another.
- A conviction does the reverse.
- Appeals to due process satisfy neither side that lost.

This is not because the losing side is irrational or dishonest. It is because the verdict instantiated an ontology they do not share.

13.6 Why Procedural Appeals Fail

After verdicts, defenders of the outcome reliably invoke:

- 'The jury heard all the evidence.'
- 'The correct legal standard was applied.'
- 'The process was fair.'

These appeals fail for structural reasons.

Procedural legitimacy operates downstream of ontological evaluation.[4]

---

3 For evidence that moral evaluation tracks prior orientation more reliably than outcome direction, see:
- Lord, C. G., Ross, L., & Lepper, M. R. (1979). Biased assimilation and attitude polarisation. *Journal of Personality and Social Psychology*.
- Taber, C. S. & Lodge, M. (2006). Motivated skepticism in the evaluation of political beliefs. *American Journal of Political Science*.
- Kunda, Z. (1990). The case for motivated reasoning. *Psychological Bulletin*.
These findings support the claim that post-decision reactions are predictable given evaluative priors, even when factual agreement is high.

4 On the limits of procedural legitimacy under evaluative disagreement, see:
- Tyler, T. R. (2006). *Why People Obey the Law*.
- Sunshine, J. & Tyler, T. R. (2003). The role of procedural justice and legitimacy in shaping public support for policing. *Law & Society Review*.
- Gibson, J. L. (200 hookup? No) Actually use: Gibson, J. L. (2007). The legitimacy of the U.S. Supreme Court. *American Political Science Review*.
These studies show that procedural fairness increases compliance and stability, but does not reliably generate moral agreement where legitimacy standards diverge upstream.

If the standard itself ('*reasonable force*') is contestable, then correct application does not resolve disagreement. It merely relocates it.

Indeed, procedural appeals often aggravate outrage by reinforcing the sense that an alien ontology has been imposed under the guise of neutrality.

13.7 The Role of Power, Explicit and Implicit

At the point of verdict, power does not enter because deliberation failed. It enters because deliberation reached its limit.

The verdict stabilises meaning temporarily. It authorises enforcement. It allows the system to move on. This is power functioning as mediator, not as corruption.

Seen this way, the legal system is not a machine for discovering justice. It is a maintenance apparatus for producing decisions under ontological plurality.

13.8 Why Reform Cycles Stall

Common reform responses – clearer statutes, better jury instructions, enhanced transparency – target downstream variables. They leave untouched the upstream divergence in salience assignment.

This is why reform cycles follow a familiar pattern:

- Outrage following verdict.
- Procedural reform proposed.
- Reform implemented.
- Next verdict produces outrage again.

The conclusion drawn is often cynicism or despair. The correct conclusion is structural misdiagnosis.

13.9 Verdicts as Maintenance, Not Resolution

Legal verdicts are best understood as maintenance events. They do not reconcile moral disagreement. They bound it.

Their success criterion is not universal acceptance but system survival: did the process produce a decision without triggering collapse, secession, or violence?

That this feels unsatisfying is not a flaw in the analysis. It is a reflection of how deeply the myth of resolution is embedded in modern legal culture.

13.10 Pattern Across Cases: Outcome Invariance and Asymmetric Outrage

The structural model advanced in this manuscript predicts a specific empirical regularity: asymmetric outrage persists regardless of outcome direction in high-salience legal cases.[5] What varies is not whether outrage occurs, but which cohort experiences it.

This pattern is not incidental. It follows directly from three features already established:

- Ontological plurality among evaluative orientations
- Institutional singularity, requiring one authoritative outcome
- Contestable action-terms (e.g., justice, legitimacy, reasonable force) that remain untethered under plural orientation

Because verdicts instantiate one orientation rather than reconciling many, dissatisfaction is structurally guaranteed.

13.10.1 Acquittals

In high-profile acquittals, one cohort experiences vindication of autonomy-centred principles such as self-defence, due process, or restraint on state punishment. Another cohort experiences moral injury grounded in harm recognition, victim legitimacy, or historical patterns of exclusion.

Despite factual convergence on events and procedures, the evaluative divide persists. Increased transparency often intensifies rather than resolves disagreement, as the same evidence is recruited to support incompatible moral conclusions.

13.10.2 Convictions

In high-profile convictions, the polarity reverses. One cohort experiences moral closure and institutional affirmation. Another experiences overreach, scapegoating, or illegitimate expansion of state power.

5 Outcome-invariant polarisation has been documented across acquittals, convictions, and negotiated outcomes in high-salience legal cases. See, e.g.,
– Haney López, I. (2014). *Dog Whistle Politics*, ch. 6 on verdict polarisation.
– Peffley, M., Hurwitz, J., & Sniderman, P. M. (1997). Racial stereotypes and whites' political views. *American Journal of Political Science*.
– Gross, S. R. et al. (2017). Race and wrongful convictions in the United States. *National Registry of Exonerations*.
These patterns persist despite variation in outcome direction, evidentiary strength, and procedural posture.

Crucially, the intensity and structure of outrage closely mirrors that observed in acquittals. The moral valence changes sign; the topology does not.

13.10.3 Settlements and Plea Agreements

Even outcomes explicitly designed to avoid binary judgment – civil settlements, plea bargains, prosecutorial discretion – do not escape the pattern. One side interprets settlement as accountability; the other as capitulation, coercion, or implicit admission of wrongdoing.

The attempt to soften singularity alters optics, not structure.[6]

13.10.4 Structural Implication

The invariance of outrage across outcome types falsifies explanations that locate persistence primarily in misinformation, irrationality, or procedural defect. If disagreement were primarily epistemic, outcomes aligned with 'the facts' would converge opinion. They do not.

Instead, the observed regularity confirms the model's prediction:

Where ontological orientations diverge, and institutions must issue singular judgments on *Contestables*, at least one cohort will experience the outcome as unjust, regardless of direction.

This is not evidence of institutional failure. It is evidence of institutional constraint.[7]

---

6 On divergent interpretations of settlements and plea bargains, see:
- Bibas, S. (2004). Plea bargaining outside the shadow of trial. *Harvard Law Review*.
- Natapoff, A. (2012). Misdemeanor justice. *Southern California Law Review*.
- Alschuler, A. W. (1979). A nearly perfect system of plea bargaining. *Journal of Criminal Law & Criminology*.

These accounts show that negotiated outcomes redistribute coercion and blame without eliminating ontological disagreement over legitimacy or harm.

7 To say that outrage is structurally invariant is not to deny the reality of harm or the importance of accountability. It is to distinguish between resolution (agreement) and maintenance (continued coordination under disagreement), and to locate law firmly in the latter category.

13.10.5 Diagnostic Value

Recognising this pattern has immediate diagnostic utility:

- It explains why reforms that increase evidence, transparency, or deliberation often fail to reduce polarisation
- It clarifies why legitimacy crises recur even when procedures are followed scrupulously
- It reframes outrage not as pathology but as a predictable by-product of plural moral architecture

The implication is not resignation, but recalibration: institutions should be designed to survive predictable dissatisfaction, not to eliminate it.

13.11 Structural Invariance Across Outcome

Legal verdicts demonstrate the full architecture of ontological conflict:

- Pre-verbal salience structures evaluation.
- Contestable concepts carry institutional force without shared grounding.
- Institutions must select one outcome.
- Power stabilises that selection.
- Outrage persists invariantly.

The verdict does not end the dispute. It suspends it.

And this is not a failure of law. It is what law looks like when language has reached its limit.

Once this is acknowledged, a further consequence follows: frameworks that seek resolution through semantic clarification, additional evidence, or idealised deliberation are methodologically mis-specified. They treat persistence as error rather than structure.

The task therefore shifts from eliminating disagreement to understanding its contours, constraints, and points of amplification. What is required is not a better argument, but a different research posture – one capable of tracking pre-verbal salience, ontological divergence, and institutional selection without presuming convergence as the default endpoint.

Chapter 14 takes up that task.

14

Methodology and Research Programme

THE PRECEDING CHAPTERS ADVANCE A STRUCTURAL CLAIM: THAT persistent moral and political disagreement in plural societies often arises not from epistemic deficit or semantic confusion, but from incompatible ontological orientations that structure pre-verbal salience assignment. Such a claim invites a predictable objection. If orientations are pre-verbal, genealogically shaped, and not directly observable, how can they be studied empirically without collapsing into speculation?

This chapter addresses that concern directly. It does not propose a single decisive experiment, nor does it attempt to reduce ontological orientation to a scalar variable. Instead, it outlines a research programme: a family of empirical strategies appropriate to structural, pre-verbal claims, together with explicit disconfirmation conditions. The aim is not to 'measure ontology' in isolation, but to test the consequences the theory predicts when ontological plurality is present.

The methodological posture adopted here is triangulatory rather than foundational.[1] No single method is decisive; convergence across methods is the evidential target. This is not a weakness of the approach. It is precisely what one should expect when the object of inquiry is pre-linguistic, distributed, and institutionally mediated.

1 Triangulation is standard where the object of inquiry is distributed, pre-reflective, or institutionally mediated. In such cases, evidential strength derives from convergence across heterogeneous methods rather than isolation of a single causal variable.

14.1 What Is (and Is Not) Being Claimed

Before outlining methods, a clarification of scope is necessary.
This framework ***does not*** claim:

- that ontological orientation is immutable,
- that individuals possess only one orientation,
- that orientations are immune to influence or acculturation,
- or that empirical convergence is impossible in principle.

It ***does*** claim that:

- orientation operates prior to linguistic articulation in salient moral domains,
- plural weighting of ontological dimensions is common in heterogeneous societies,
- certain action-authorising terms remain structurally unstable under such plurality,
- and institutional decision-points force singular outcomes regardless.

Accordingly, the empirical question is not whether people can change their views, but whether semantic clarification, procedural refinement, or increased information reliably produce convergence once disputes occupy the *Contestables/Fluids* boundary. The framework predicts that they often will not.

Like intersectional frameworks, the present model rejects single-axis explanation. Unlike additive or hierarchical approaches, however, it does not attempt to decompose outcomes into contributory identity variables. Ontological orientations interact non-linearly, shift in salience by context, and resist stable ordering. The framework therefore does not seek to explain behaviour through identity accounting, but to explain the persistence of incompatible justifications once factual convergence has occurred. Ontological orientations operate as structured propensities that shape salience and justificatory stability, not as behavioural signatures. What remains stable across contexts is not action, but the hierarchy of reasons that survive interpretive stress.

14.2 Behavioural Proxies for Ontological Orientation

Ontological orientation is not directly observable.[2] Its presence must therefore be inferred from behavioural regularities under controlled variation.

Candidate proxies include:

Threat detection asymmetries

Differential perception of danger in identical scenarios (e.g., armed vs unarmed presence, crowd dynamics, authority challenges).

Authority compliance thresholds

Variation in perceived legitimacy of commands, rules, or enforcement actions under matched factual conditions.

Harm prioritisation patterns

Divergent assessments of whose harm 'counts', whose suffering is salient, and which losses are morally tolerable.

Agency and responsibility attribution

Systematic differences in assigning blame, intent, or victimhood when factual narratives are held constant.

Crucially, these proxies do not presuppose shared semantics. They track pre-reflective responses and downstream justifications, allowing orientation to be inferred from stable patterns rather than self-report alone.

14.3 Narrative Elicitation and Salience Mapping

Narrative methods are particularly well-suited to this framework because they reveal what agents spontaneously foreground, omit, or background when recounting the same event.

Approaches include:

- open-ended narrative reconstruction of shared stimuli,
- comparison of first-pass vs reflective explanations,
- analysis of which elements are treated as morally decisive rather than merely descriptive.

2 The use of behavioural proxies here is inferential rather than psychometric. The aim is not to classify individuals, but to detect stable divergence patterns under controlled variation. Orientation is inferred from response regularities, not measured as a latent trait.

Patterns of divergence here are diagnostic. The framework predicts that even when factual recall converges, salience profiles will not, and that subsequent moral language will track those profiles rather than correct them.

Narrative elicitation thus functions as a bridge between pre-verbal salience and explicit moral judgement.

14.4 Translation Stress Tests

One of the most powerful diagnostic tools proposed is the translation stress test.[3]

The procedure is simple:

- Present an identical event description to multiple cohorts.
- Require participants to translate their moral judgement into an alternative normative vocabulary (legal, utilitarian, rights-based, procedural).
- Measure degradation, distortion, or resistance during translation.
- The framework predicts that:
- Invariant claims translate cleanly.
- Contestables exhibit repair attempts, metaphor substitution, or outright refusal.
- Increased pressure to translate intensifies frustration rather than convergence.

This approach directly tests the Language Insufficiency Hypothesis *in situ*, revealing where semantic substitution fails despite shared intent to communicate.

3 Translation stress tests operationalise the Language Insufficiency Hypothesis by forcing semantic substitution under shared intent. Failure modes – repair attempts, metaphor proliferation, refusal – are treated as data rather than noise.

14.5 Triangulation Across Methods

No single method is sufficient. The strength of the programme lies in convergent failure across distinct empirical approaches.

When:

- behavioural proxies diverge,
- narrative salience profiles remain stable within cohorts,
- translation attempts degrade,
- and institutional outcomes trigger asymmetric outrage despite procedural legitimacy,
- the most parsimonious explanation is not ignorance or bad faith, but ontological divergence.

Triangulation here functions not to '*prove*' ontology, but to eliminate competing explanations that would predict convergence under these conditions.

14.6 Falsifiability and Disconfirmation Conditions

The framework is explicitly falsifiable.[4] It would be seriously undermined by robust evidence of any of the following:

1. **Durable convergence on Contestables**
   Persistent agreement on action-authorising terms (e.g., justice, legitimacy, reasonable force) across plural cohorts without coercion or exclusion.

2. **Semantic repair success at high complexity**
   Reliable resolution of moral conflict through clarification, reframing, or dialogue alone once disputes exceed the Invariant domain.

3. **Institutional outcomes experienced as just across incompatible orientations**
   Singular decisions that consistently generate cross-cohort legitimacy in high-stakes cases.

4 Disconfirmation conditions are structural rather than anecdotal. The framework would be undermined by systematic evidence of durable convergence on action-authorising terms under plural ontology without coercion, exclusion, or engineered homogeneity.

4. **Elimination of asymmetric outrage through procedural optimisation**
   Demonstrated collapse of post-decision divergence via improved process design alone.

If such patterns were observed systematically rather than episodically, the core structural claim would require revision or abandonment.

14.7 Implications for Institutional Research

This research programme has direct implications for how institutions are studied and evaluated.

Rather than asking whether a decision was objectively correct, the framework recommends asking:

- which ontological orientations were instantiated,
- which were negated,
- how loss was distributed,
- and whether variance was damped without erasure.

Institutional success, on this view, is not measured by consensus but by containment: reduced escalation, predictable application of power, and avoidance of catastrophic failure under pluralism.

14.8 Summary

This chapter has outlined an empirical posture appropriate to pre-verbal, structural claims. The framework does not retreat from testability; it insists on the right kind of test.

Ontological orientation cannot be isolated like a hormone level, but its effects can be traced, predicted, and, crucially, failed. Where disagreement persists despite shared facts, good faith, and procedural legitimacy, the framework predicts structural divergence. Where such divergence disappears, the framework stands corrected.

The ambition, then, is modest but non-negotiable: not to resolve pluralism, but to understand its mechanics well enough to stop mistaking inevitability for failure.

15

Limits, Reflexivity, and Ontological Disclosure

Any framework that claims to diagnose structural limits will inevitably face a reflexive challenge: does the diagnosis itself escape the limits it describes? If not, why should it be taken seriously rather than dismissed as another partisan construction?

This chapter addresses that challenge directly. Not by denying it, but by incorporating it.

15.1 This Is Not a View from Nowhere

This work does not claim ontological neutrality.[1] It does not pretend to speak from outside the space it maps. That expectation belongs to the very Enlightenment inheritance under critique.

The framework advanced here is itself situated. It is shaped by a particular weighting of dimensions: scepticism toward moral realism, resistance to teleological resolution, discomfort with coercive authority masked as consensus, and an emphasis on structural explanation over normative proclamation Stating this is not a concession. It is a methodological requirement.

Ontological disclosure does not invalidate analysis; it makes it legible. Pretending otherwise merely smuggles priors in under the banner of objectivity.

1 Claims to neutrality function historically as masking devices for inherited ontological commitments. Disclosure here is methodological rather than confessional: it renders evaluative priors visible so that their effects can be assessed rather than denied.

15.2 Why This Is Not Relativism in the Pejorative Sense

The most common objection is predictable: if moral judgments are ontologically indexed, does anything go? Is every outcome as good as any other?

No. And the reason is structural, not moral.

First, this framework does not deny constraint. Outcomes are bounded by:

- material reality
- institutional design
- historical path dependence
- asymmetric power distribution
- the cost of enforcement

Second, it does not deny harm. It explains why harm recognition itself diverges.

Third, it does not deny critique. It relocates it.

Critique does not proceed by claiming access to the true meaning of justice. It proceeds by asking different questions:

- Which ontology is being instantiated?
- Who bears the cost?
- How stable is the arrangement?
- How much coercion is required to maintain it?
- What failure modes does it create?

This is not relativism as indifference. It is relativism as diagnostic realism.[2]

---

2 The position defended here aligns with structural rather than normative relativism: it locates variability in conditions of justification rather than in the permissibility of outcomes. Constraint, harm, and enforceability remain operative even where universal moral grounding is unavailable.

15.3 Nor Is This Quietism

Another charge follows close behind: if resolution is structurally unavailable, why act at all? This misunderstands the claim.

The framework does not say action is futile. It says certain kinds of action are misdirected.

Specifically, it rejects the idea that:

- better arguments
- clearer definitions
- moral exhortation
- semantic repair

can reconcile ontological divergence. What remains is not paralysis but maintenance.

Action shifts from persuasion to design. From convergence to containment. From moral victory to loss minimisation.

Quietism would be disengagement. This is the opposite: it demands more disciplined institutional thinking and fewer comforting myths.

15.4 Moral Realism as an Ontological Vector

The framework can also accommodate moral realism without granting it special privilege.

For those who experience moral facts as discovered rather than constructed, this is treated as an ontological orientation with a distinctive pre-verbal vector: moral salience is perceived as emanating from the world rather than from social coordination.[3]

Nothing in the model forbids this. What it denies is that such perception is universally binding.

When moral realism collides with non-realist orientations, the resulting conflict behaves exactly as predicted: semantic appeals to truth fail; institutional power selects; outrage follows.

The disagreement is not about whether moral facts exist. It is about whether their existence settles political legitimacy. Structurally, it does not.

---

3 Compare Bernard Williams, *Ethics and the Limits of Philosophy* (1985), on the fragility of moral objectivity, though Williams stops short of treating institutional outcomes as necessarily exclusionary instantiations of value.

15.5 Why Science Is Not a Counterexample Revisited

At this point, it is worth restating why scientific convergence does not refute the argument.

Science achieves partial convergence because it operates under unusually restrictive conditions:

- ontological variance is filtered by training and selection
- interpretation is disciplined by material coupling
- error is penalised by predictive failure
- institutions reward alignment over plural legitimacy

Even then, convergence is local, provisional, and fragile.

The hostile reception of Kuhn, Feyerabend, and Latour was not philosophical disagreement alone. It was an immune response to exposure of stabilising mechanisms long mistaken for epistemic inevitability. Science converges where ontology is constrained. Politics does not.

15.6 What This Framework Cannot Do

Intellectual honesty requires boundary marking.

This framework does not:

- tell you which ontology is correct
- adjudicate moral truth
- predict the timing of conflict
- eliminate the need for judgment
- provide a blueprint for justice

It explains why these expectations are misplaced. If this feels unsatisfying, that dissatisfaction is not accidental. It reflects the gap between what modern political theory promises and what plural societies can structurally sustain.

15.7 Why Strengthens, Not Weakens, the Argument

Admitting one's ontological position does not collapse the framework into autobiography.[4]

On the contrary, it demonstrates confidence in the model's generality. The argument does not depend on readers sharing the author's orientation. It depends on readers recognising the pattern when orientations collide.

If you reject this framework, you must say where.

- Do you deny ontological plurality?
- Do you deny pre-verbal salience?
- Do you deny contestability at high complexity?
- Do you deny institutional singularity?
- Do you deny the role of power in stabilisation?

Anything else is rhetoric.

15.8 The Closing Claim

This work does not argue that justice is impossible. It argues that justice is not singular.

It does not claim power is good. It claims power is unavoidable when language runs out.

It does not promise peace. It promises a clearer account of why peace is fragile.

Where semantic reconciliation is structurally unavailable, institutional power does not corrupt politics. It is politics. The task is not to abolish this fact, but to design systems that survive it without demanding belief in a unity that does not exist. That is not a comforting conclusion. It is, however, a more honest one.

---

4 Reflexive disclosure does not exempt a framework from critique; it intensifies it. By making its own ontological commitments explicit, the framework invites challenge at the correct structural level rather than at the level of presumed neutrality.

When Language Fails: A Closing Argument

THIS MANUSCRIPT BEGAN WITH A MODEST CLAIM AND FOLLOWED it to an uncomfortable conclusion.

The modest claim was that persistent moral and political disagreement is not primarily a failure of information, intelligence, or good faith. It is the predictable outcome of ontological plurality operating under conditions of high conceptual complexity.

The uncomfortable conclusion is that no amount of semantic refinement can resolve this condition, and that institutions do not reconcile disagreement so much as terminate it. Everything else follows.

16.1 The Enlightenment Promise, Reconsidered

Modern political and moral theory inherits a promise, often unstated but deeply felt: that disagreement is a transitional phase. That with enough education, dialogue, data, or deliberation, convergence is the natural end state.

This promise animates:

- deliberative democracy
- evidence-based policy
- moral persuasion strategies
- rational-choice institutional design
- bridge-building programmes premised on mutual understanding

What this work has argued is not that these efforts are naïve, but that they are mis-scoped. They assume a level of ontological alignment that does not exist and, in many domains, cannot exist.

The error is not optimism. It is category confusion.[1]

16.2 Why Better Arguments Fail Predictably

Across science, policing, law, and public morality, the same pattern appears:

- factual convergence is often achievable
- interpretive convergence is not
- Contestables remain untethered
- institutions must still act

When outcomes diverge despite shared facts, the reflex is to demand better reasoning. This manuscript has argued that such demands arrive too late in the causal chain.

By the time arguments are exchanged, salience has already been assigned, roles allocated, and legitimacy conferred or denied. Language does not fail because it is vague. It fails because it is downstream.

16.3 Institutions as Collapse Mechanisms

Institutions exist to do what plural societies cannot: decide. They collapse multidimensional disagreement into a single outcome. They do so not by discovering truth, but by exercising authorised power under procedural constraints. This is not a moral accusation. It is a functional description.

Courts do not resolve justice. They issue verdicts. Police do not settle legitimacy. They enforce order. Scientific institutions do not reveal reality in toto. They stabilise models sufficient for action.

The outrage that follows institutional decisions is not evidence of malfunction. It is evidence that collapse has occurred.

1 The promise of eventual convergence through reason is not rejected as false in principle, but as misapplied to domains characterised by irreducible ontological plurality. Where background salience structures diverge, convergence cannot be assumed without prior homogenisation.

16.4 Power Without Romance

A recurring temptation is to treat power as a moral contaminant. Something that enters only when the process has failed. This manuscript rejects that story.

Power is what operates when semantic resources are exhausted.[2] It is not the opposite of reason; it is what replaces reason when reasons no longer bind.

The question is therefore not how to eliminate power, but how to structure it:

- visibly rather than covertly
- predictably rather than arbitrarily
- reversibly rather than permanently
- with distributed rather than concentrated loss

That is a design problem, not a rhetorical one.

16.5 What This Framework Offers Instead

This work does not offer reconciliation. It offers orientation.

It allows us to:

- predict where disagreement will persist
- distinguish epistemic disputes from ontological ones
- identify when dialogue is likely to fail
- understand why reforms stall despite good intentions
- design institutions for durability rather than harmony

If that feels austere, it is because the alternative has been indulgent.

16.6 The Final Provocation

If even scientific communities, operating under extreme material constraint and institutional discipline, achieve convergence only by suppressing ontological plurality through selection and acculturation, then expecting moral or political convergence through better talk is not hopeful. It is incoherent.

---

2 Power is treated here descriptively rather than normatively: as the mechanism by which institutions stabilise coordination when reasons fail to bind across plural orientations. This does not entail endorsement of any particular distribution of power.

Pluralism is not a temporary defect. It is a permanent condition.

Language is not the master tool of social coordination. It is one instrument among others, and it has limits.

Justice is not a destination. It is a contested terrain that institutions traverse by force of authority, not force of argument.

The task, then, is not to finish the argument. It is to build systems that survive its failure.

Appendix

Empirical Anchors, Scope Conditions, and Disconfirmation Criteria

A0. Purpose and Status of This Appendix

The framework advanced here does not deny the existence of epistemic disagreement, strategic misrepresentation, or bad-faith actors. Nor does it claim that all conflict is ontological in origin. Rather, it identifies a specific and recurrent failure mode: high-stakes, identity-loaded, action-authorising disputes that persist after factual clarification and procedural integrity. In domains where disagreement collapses under shared evidence, incentive alignment, or semantic repair, standard epistemic or strategic models remain sufficient and are not challenged by this account.

This appendix serves three functions:

To demonstrate that the manuscript's claims are empirically legible, not merely speculative.

To clarify where the ontological model applies most forcefully, and where standard epistemic or strategic explanations suffice.

To specify what kinds of empirical findings would disconfirm or constrain the model.

The appendix is not intended as an exhaustive literature review, nor as a proof of the thesis by accumulation of studies. Its role is diagnostic and orienting: to show that the structural claims advanced in the manuscript align with well-documented empirical patterns, and to mark their limits.

A1. Pre-Verbal Salience and Moral Judgment

Indexed claim:

Salience, threat recognition, and moral evaluation occur prior to conscious reasoning and linguistic articulation.

Relevant literatures:

- Haidt, *The Emotional Dog and Its Rational Tail* (2001)
- Greene et al., *fMRI studies on trolley problems* (2001–2014)
- Bargh et al. on automaticity and moral priming
- Cushman et al. on harm, intent, and moral cognition timing

Representative findings:

A substantial body of work shows that moral evaluations are initiated rapidly and often pre-consciously, with affective and intuitive responses preceding articulated justification. Subjects routinely confabulate reasons post hoc whilst maintaining high confidence in their judgments. Manipulations of affect, framing, or priming reliably alter salience without producing durable convergence in moral assessment.

Key empirical regularities:

- Moral judgments are reliably formed within milliseconds of stimulus exposure.
- Post-hoc reasoning tracks prior affective response rather than determining it.
- Cross-group differences persist even under identical informational exposure.

Interpretive relevance:

These findings support the manuscript's distinction between genealogical formation (how orientations develop) and operational priority (how they function in the moment). They do not imply irrationality or pathology, only that reasoning is downstream.

A2. Persistence After Factual Convergence

Indexed claim:

In high-salience moral and political conflicts, disagreement frequently persists after factual clarification and procedural integrity.

Relevant domains:

High-profile legal verdicts, policing incidents with video evidence, politically salient scientific disputes.

Representative literatures:

- Lakoff on framing and metaphor activation
- Fernbach et al., 'The Illusion of Explanatory Depth'
- Nyhan & Reifler on motivated reasoning
- Sunstein on group polarisation

Observed pattern:

- Individuals report increased confidence after explanation without increased accuracy.
- Framing interventions succeed in low-complexity domains but plateau or backfire in identity-loaded disputes.
- Dialogue increases articulation, not alignment, once Contestables dominate.

Representative findings:

Across multiple contexts, opposing cohorts often converge on descriptive facts whilst continuing to diverge sharply on evaluative conclusions. Post-verdict surveys routinely show stable polarisation irrespective of outcome direction. Additional evidence exposure frequently intensifies confidence and moral condemnation rather than dampening it.

Interpretive significance:

These patterns are inconsistent with models that locate persistence primarily in misinformation or epistemic deficit. They support the claim that Contestables remain structurally untethered even as Invariants expand.

A3. Transparency and Body-Camera Effects

Indexed claim:

Expanding access to observables increases agreement on Invariants whilst leaving Contestables structurally underdetermined.

Empirical touchpoints:

- Post-verdict opinion surveys in high-profile trials
- Body-camera interpretation studies (e.g. Morrow et al.)
- Experimental vignettes showing stable divergence in 'reasonable force' judgments

Key regularity:

- Disagreement persists after facts are shared and procedures acknowledged as valid.
- Divergence tracks identity and authority orientation more strongly than information access.

Relevant literatures:

Criminal justice reform, transparency and accountability studies, media interpretation research.

Representative findings:

Body-camera footage and similar transparency interventions reliably increase agreement on sequences of events, timing, and observable actions. However, interpretations of threat, proportionality, intent, and reasonableness remain sharply divided. The same footage is routinely cited by opposing sides as confirming incompatible judgments.

Interpretive significance:

These findings illustrate the Language Insufficiency Hypothesis in situ. Transparency improves descriptive alignment but does not resolve action-authorising disagreement. The failure mode is structural, not procedural.

A4. Scientific Convergence as Engineered Homogeneity

Indexed claim:

Scientific convergence is not a baseline human capacity but an engineered outcome under restrictive institutional conditions.

Representative literatures:

- Kuhn on paradigms and normal science
- Replication crisis meta-analyses
- Sociologies of peer review and disciplinary gatekeeping
- Studies of interdisciplinary friction (e.g. econ vs sociology; neuroscience vs psychology)

Observed pattern:

- Convergence correlates with training pipelines, methodological exclusion, and incentive alignment.
- Disputes intensify at disciplinary boundaries where ontological assumptions diverge.

Representative findings:

Convergence increases where selection, shared training, replication pressure, and material constraint discipline interpretation. At theoretical and interdisciplinary boundaries, pluralism re-emerges despite shared datasets. High-prestige disputes persist where adequacy criteria diverge.

Illustrative cases:

Debates in consciousness research and nature–nurture disputes in behavioural science demonstrate shared evidence combined with incompatible explanatory priorities.

Interpretive significance:

Science functions as a confirming instance of the model rather than a counterexample. Where ontological variance is reduced and material coupling is strong, convergence is achievable. Where these conditions lapse, the predicted fracture appears.

A.5 Scope Conditions: When the Ontological Model Applies – and When It Doesn't

The manuscript does not claim:

- That all disagreement is ontological
- That bad faith never occurs
- That misinformation is irrelevant
- That communication is never effective

The ontological model applies most forcefully where disputes are:

- High-stakes
- Identity-load-bearing
- Action-authorising
- Persistent after clarification
- Escalatory under increased contact

By contrast, epistemic or strategic models suffice where:

- Stakes are low or instrumental
- Concepts are tightly tethered to observables
- Incentives dominate over identity
- Disagreement collapses under shared evidence

Additional Scope Clarifications:

The framework does not claim that ontological orientations generate invariant behavioural outputs or that intersecting identity dimensions can be cleanly decomposed. Agents operate across multiple ontological fault-lines simultaneously, with weightings that vary by domain (sex, gender, religion, economics, authority). This produces propensities rather than signatures – making clean causal attribution structurally impossible. The model's explanatory target is not 'why did this person act this way' but 'why does this justification remain legitimate to one cohort and obscene to another after factual convergence'.

Similarly, the framework acknowledges that 'reason', 'rationality', and 'evidence' are themselves ontologically indexed rather than neutral. Different orientations support internally coherent but mutually irreducible forms of reasoning. This is not relativism but structural pluralism: logic operates perfectly within each ontology whilst remaining unable to adjudicate between them.

A6. Translation Stress and Cross-Orientation Failure

Indexed claim:

Attempts to translate action-authorising terms across ontological orientations reliably fail without coercive settlement.

Relevant methods:

Cross-cultural vignette studies, narrative elicitation, moral translation tasks.

Representative findings:

Participants frequently report 'understanding' opposing positions whilst continuing to reject their legitimacy. Lexical translation succeeds, but action-authorising force does not transfer. Increased exposure and dialogue do not reliably produce convergence in high-salience contexts.

Interpretive significance:

These results support the distinction between lexical overlap and ontological alignment. Communication may occur without convergence, and often without even mutual recognitional symmetry.

A7. Illustrative Toy Design: Translation Stress Under Ontological Plurality

Purpose.

This illustrative design demonstrates how ontological divergence might be empirically probed without presupposing fixed group taxonomies or treating disagreement as epistemic error. It is not a proposed experiment, but a schematic showing what empirical engagement with the framework could look like.

Step 1: Case Selection

Select a single high-salience, action-authorising case with:

- agreed descriptive facts,
- persistent evaluative disagreement.

Example cases:

- a police shooting with body-camera footage,
- a controversial legal verdict,
- a climate policy trade-off involving economic harm.

Step 2: Factual Convergence Check

Participants are first asked to answer factual questions about the case:

- sequence of events,
- observable actions,
- legal or procedural facts.

Participants who fail to converge on these are excluded from further analysis.

(This step isolates epistemic disagreement from ontological divergence.)

Step 3: Translation Task

Participants are then presented with paired justifications:

- one aligned with their own evaluative judgment,
- one aligned with an opposing judgment.

They are asked:

- whether they understand the opposing justification,
- whether they regard it as legitimate,
- whether it could justify the action taken.

Crucially, participants are not asked to change their judgment.

Step 4: Stress Manipulation

The same justification is re-presented under:

- alternative framings,
- increased contextual detail,
- explicit acknowledgement of trade-offs.

Confidence, legitimacy attribution, and affective response are measured across iterations.

Predicted Outcome (Framework Index)

The model predicts:

- high reported understanding without legitimacy transfer,
- stable evaluative judgments despite increased information,
- affective amplification rather than convergence under stress.

Disconfirmation and Scope Constraints

The framework would be challenged if:

- legitimacy attribution reliably increases across iterations,
- evaluative judgments converge without coercion,
- framing effects produce durable cross-orientation agreement in action-authorising judgments.

Interpretive Note.

A null result here would not imply irrationality or bad faith. It would indicate that semantic translation and factual alignment are insufficient to bridge ontological divergence in high-stakes contexts – precisely the structural claim of the manuscript.

Closing Note

This appendix does not claim empirical closure. It establishes empirical legibility. The framework advanced in the manuscript tracks existing evidence more closely than prevailing semantic, epistemic, or procedural accounts, and it generates testable predictions about where and why convergence will fail.

Future work may refine, formalise, or revise the model. The present aim is narrower: to show that persistent moral conflict is already better explained by ontological plurality than by failures of information, language, or goodwill.

Language has not failed because we have not tried hard enough. It has failed because we keep asking it to do work it cannot structurally perform.

Unfortunate. Predictable. Documented.

That should do.

Glossary of Terms

Action-Authorising Term

A concept whose invocation licenses or justifies action, often coercive or exclusionary (e.g., justice, legitimacy, reasonable force). Such terms do not merely describe states of affairs but function to authorise decisions, sanctions, or interventions.

Asymmetric Outrage

The predictable persistence of moral condemnation or grievance following an institutional decision, where different cohorts experience the same outcome as either vindication or injustice. Asymmetry refers to the distribution of outrage across ontological orientations, not to intensity alone.

Contestables

Concepts that appear determinate in ordinary use but lack shared ontological grounding under plural orientation. Contestables are:

- distant from direct observables,
- dependent on thick ethical judgments,
- identity- or legitimacy-loaded,
- and action-authorising.

They contrast with Invariants (tightly tethered to shared observables) and Ineffables (beyond stable articulation).

Effectiveness Horizon (Language)

The point along the complexity gradient at which linguistic communication ceases to reliably coordinate understanding or action across agents. Beyond this horizon, increased clarification or dialogue may intensify disagreement rather than resolve it.

Genealogical Formation

The historical, cultural, institutional, and developmental processes through which an agent's ontological orientation is shaped. Genealogy explains how orientations arise; it does not determine how they operate in real time.

Institutional Singularity (or Singularity Machine)
The structural property of institutions whereby plural inputs (interpretations, claims, orientations) must be collapsed into a single authoritative output (verdict, policy, ruling). Singularity is a functional constraint, not a normative ideal.

Invariants
Concepts or claims that remain tightly tethered to shared perceptual reference, procedure, or measurement, allowing high levels of cross-agent agreement (e.g., timing of events, physical sequences, numerical counts).

Language Insufficiency Hypothesis (LIH)
The claim that as conceptual complexity increases, the effectiveness of language in coordinating understanding and action decreases, even as perceived effectiveness often remains high. LIH explains why semantic repair can fail systematically in high-stakes domains.

Maintenance (Institutional)
An alternative design objective to resolution. Maintenance aims to stabilise coordination under persistent disagreement through variance damping, loss distribution, rotation, exit options, and procedural durability, rather than convergence on shared justification.

Ontological Orientation
A pre-verbally operative world-relation that structures salience, threat recognition, authority, autonomy, harm attribution, and legitimacy prior to linguistic reasoning. Ontological orientation is not a belief set, value list, or ideology, though it conditions all three.

Operational Priority
The fact that ontological orientation functions before conscious reasoning or linguistic articulation in evaluative judgment. Reasons typically follow salience assignment rather than determine it.

Power (Hard / Soft / Structural)

Forms of mediation that stabilise meaning or coordination when semantic reconciliation is unavailable:

- Hard power: coercive settlement of acute events.
- Soft power: norm-setting, agenda control, and legitimacy shaping.
- Structural power: path dependence and institutional inertia.
- Presumption Gap

The divergence between perceived mutual understanding and actual ontological alignment. Agents presume successful communication because lexical overlap exists, even when underlying action-authorising commitments diverge.

Resolution

The ideal of convergence on shared justification or agreement. The manuscript treats resolution as achievable in low-complexity domains but structurally unavailable in many high-stakes, identity-loaded contexts.

Semantic Layer

The level at which meanings, interpretations, and justifications are articulated and contested. Semantic disagreement is often downstream of ontological divergence.

Translation Stress Test

An empirical or diagnostic method for probing ontological divergence by examining whether understanding transfers into legitimacy attribution or action endorsement under increased framing, clarification, or contextual detail.

Untethering (Ontological)

The condition in which a concept lacks a shared grounding in perceptual reference, procedure, or material constraint, despite appearing determinate in use. Untethering explains why Contestables can function authoritatively without convergence.

Select Bibliography

I. Ontological Orientation, Pre-Verbal Judgment, and Moral Psychology

These empirically ground operational priority without endorsing the semantic optimism we later diagnose as misplaced.

Haidt, J. (2001). The emotional dog and its rational tail: A social intuitionist approach to moral judgment. *Psychological Review,* 108(4), 814–834.

Haidt, J. (2012). *The Righteous Mind: Why Good People Are Divided by Politics and Religion*. Pantheon.

Greene, J. (2013). *Moral Tribes: Emotion, Reason, and the Gap Between Us and Them*. Penguin.

Greene, J., Sommerville, R., Nystrom, L., Darley, J., & Cohen, J. (2001). An fMRI investigation of emotional engagement in moral judgment. *Science*, 293(5537), 2105–2108.

Gray, K., Young, L., & Waytz, A. (2012). Mind perception is the essence of morality. *Psychological Inquiry*, 23(2), 101–124.

Kahneman, D. (2011). *Thinking, Fast and Slow*. Farrar, Straus and Giroux.

II. Language, Contestation, and Conceptual Indeterminacy

These establish that contestation is not a defect but a structural feature of certain concepts, which we then relocate ontologically.

Gallie, W. B. (1956). Essentially contested concepts. *Proceedings of the Aristotelian Society*, 56, 167–198.

Wittgenstein, L. (1953). *Philosophical Investigations*. Blackwell.

Williams, B. (1985). *Ethics and the Limits of Philosophy*. Harvard University Press.

Putnam, H. (1975). The meaning of 'meaning'. *In Mind, Language and Reality*. Cambridge University Press.

III. Language Insufficiency, Framing, and the Limits of Semantic Repair

These document framing effects and semantic activation whilst tacitly assuming convergence is possible if done correctly. The thesis specifies the boundary where that hope collapses.

Lakoff, G. (2016/1996). *Moral Politics: How Liberals and Conservatives Think*. University of Chicago Press.

Lakoff, G., & Johnson, M. (1980). *Metaphors We Live By*. University of Chicago Press.

Pinker, S. (2007). *The Stuff of Thought*. Viking.

IV. Science, Incommensurability, and Engineered Convergence

These show that convergence is conditional, policed, and institutional, not the default outcome of rational inquiry.

Kuhn, T. S. (1962). *The Structure of Scientific Revolutions*. University of Chicago Press.

Feyerabend, P. (1975). *Against Method*. Verso.

Latour, B., & Woolgar, S. (1979). *Laboratory Life*. Princeton University Press.

Longino, H. (1990). *Science as Social Knowledge*. Princeton University Press.

Ioannidis, J. (2005). Why most published research findings are false. *PLoS Medicine*, 2(8), e124.

V. Law, Policing, and Institutional Judgment

These empirically document legitimacy, asymmetry, and interpretation variance without needing the ontological diagnosis to be sympathetic.

Tyler, T. (2006). *Why People Obey the Law*. Princeton University Press.

Kahan, D. (2012). Cultural cognition as a conception of the cultural theory of risk. In Roeser et al. (Eds.), *Handbook of Risk Theory*. Springer.

Harris, D. (2010). *The Stories, the Statistics, and the Law*. University of Michigan Press.

Silbey, S. (2005). After legal consciousness. *Annual Review of Law and Social Science*, 1, 323–368.

VI. Liberal Proceduralism and Its Scope Conditions

These allow us to say, cleanly and defensibly: this works under shared ontological conditions; pluralism breaks the machinery.

Rawls, J. (1971). *A Theory of Justice*. Harvard University Press.

Rawls, J. (1993). *Political Liberalism*. Columbia University Press.

Habermas, J. (1984). *The Theory of Communicative Action,* Vol. 1. Beacon Press.

Habermas, J. (1996). *Between Facts and Norms*. MIT Press.

VII. Power, Institutions, and Structural Mediation

These frame power as stabilisation, selection, and constraint rather than merely malice or domination.

Foucault, M. (1977). *Discipline and Punish*. Vintage.

Foucault, M. (1980). *Power/Knowledge*. Pantheon.

Lukes, S. (2005). *Power: A Radical View*. Palgrave.

Scott, J. C. (1998). *Seeing Like a State*. Yale University Press.

VIII. Design, Pluralism, and Maintenance

These demonstrate that pluralism has always been managed institutionally, never resolved philosophically.

Ostrom, E. (1990). *Governing the Commons*. Cambridge University Press.

Lijphart, A. (1977). *Democracy in Plural Societies*. Yale University Press.

Sunstein, C. (2002). *The Law of Group Polarization*. Journal of Political Philosophy, 10(2), 175–195.

IX. Author's Prior Work and Related Frameworks

Willis, B. (2026). *Language Insufficiency Hypothesis*. Philosophics Press.

Willis, B. (2025). The Mediated Encounter Ontology of the World: A Relational Metaphysics Beyond Mind and World. Zenodo. https://doi.org/10.5281/zenodo.17685689

Willis, B. (2025). Language As Interface: Underconstraint, Genealogy, and Moral Incommensurability. Zenodo. https://doi.org/10.5281/zenodo.18181954

Willis, B. (2025). The Fact of the Matter: After Bernard Williams – Truthfulness, Facts, and the Myth of Immediacy. Zenodo. https://doi.org/10.5281/zenodo.18133958

Willis, B. (2026). Grammatical Failure: Why Liberal Epistemology Cannot Diagnose Indoctrination. Zenodo. https://doi.org/10.5281/zenodo.18521457

Willis, B. (2026). Illegible Futures: Affective Legibility and the Governance of Optimism. Zenodo. https://doi.org/10.5281/zenodo.18501335

This bibliography is selective rather than exhaustive. It reflects works that directly inform the manuscript's diagnostic framework rather than the full range of positions it critiques.

Index

A

acculturation 42, 46–47, 55, 59–61, 69, 82, 102
acculturation in policing 42
acculturation in scientific communities 117
acculturation police institutions 80
acquittals 28, 64, 67, 91, 95, 97–98
action-authorising
action-authorising conflicts 3
action-authorising Contestables 92
action-authorising, convergence 75
action-authorising force 28
action-authorising roles 23
action-authorising terms 1, 22
durble convergence 105
structurally unstable 102
untethered Contestables 85
affective polarisation 79
animal spirits 2
appeal
appeal to better intentions (insufficient) 37
appeal to better reasoning 80
appeal to better training 82
appeal to clearer language (insufficient) 37, 80
appeal to clearer standards 82
appeal to due process 91, 95
appeal to empathy 17
appeal to evidence 91
appeal to improved deliberation (insufficient) 37
appeal to instructions 91
appeal to jury trials (failure) 67
appeal to more dialogue 82
appeal to precedent doesn't stablise meaning 24
appeal to reason 17
appeal to scientific norms 51
appeal to shared standards 22, 73
appeal to shared values 17
procedural appeals aggravate outrage 96
procedural appeals as low complexity 15

procedural appeals, why they fail 95
semantic appeals to truth 111
arbiters, neutral 27
assimilation as non-neutral policy 88
asymmetric harm recognition 2
asymmetric incomprehension 17
asymmetric losses 81
asymmetric outrage 2, 29
authoritarianism 55
authority
legitimated use of force by authority 62
stabilisation by institutional authority 65

B

bad faith 75, 79
bad faith and failure 29
behavioural interventions 53–54
behavioural measures 49
behavioural proxies 103
behavioural signatures 102
better arguments (why they fail) 116
better intentions, insufficiency 37
body cameras 62–63

C

cannabis legalisation (case) 86
capitalism 82
capture 79
category error 25, 49, 79, 83, 85
charter schools 87
civilian testimony (in policing) 61
clearer language (insufficiency) 37
cognitive linguistics 3
cognitive resources, finite 50
coherence maintenance (as homogeneity gate) 48
command presence, prioritisation (in policing) 60
communicative rationality 75, 79
complex disease aetiology 53–54
computational models 49
conflicts 23
moral conflicts 2
political conflicts 2
consciousness research 49, 53–54

constraints
acknowledgement of constraints (maintenance) 88
awarenesss of asymmetric agency constraints 4
constraint density 68
constraints of democratic institutions 80
constraints on institutions 13
constraints on ontological collision
consciousness research (case) 49–50
constraints on power
material coupling, replication, engineering 41
constraints on power (maintenance) 81
constraints on scientific authority 52
experimental constraints 54
external constraints (in science)
material coupling as discipline 48–49
replication, prediction, function 45
institutional constraints
convergence 57
IQ (case) 51
legal verdicts 98–99
singularity 80
interpretive constraints (in moral realism) 13
justice, renegotiation under constraint 77
material constraints (in policing) 59
material constraints (in science) 42, 53, 117
material coupling constraints (in science)
discipline 55
table entry 69
model constraints 34–36
ontological constraints (morality, relativism) 110
operative constraints (for ontological plurality) 3
procedural constraints 116
subordinate to personal meaning (in science) 47
resolution through constraints (in science) 50
selection constraints (in policing) 68
shared constraints (in science) 47
singularity constraints (in institutions) 29
special constraints (in science) 56
stabilising constraints (in science) 57
structural constraints (institutions) 27
structural constraints (model) 33
structural constraints (power) 18
structural reality constraints (in policing)
table entry 70

structural reality constraints (in science)
table entry 70
world pushes back 48
containment 86
contestability
structural criteria for 22
Contestables 17–18, 21–26, 50, 54–55, 57, 64–69
action-authorising Contestables 85
Contestables and body cameras 62
Contestables and Fluids 16
boundary 102
Contestables and legal judgment 92, 98
Contestables in institutions and politics 24
Contestables (in policing) 67
durable convergence 105
historical patterns 116
power and semantic failure 41
translation stress test 104
untethered Contestables 1, 21
contestable terms 56
contested judgments 42
contingency reduction 36
controversies 53–54
convergence 51
by communication 75
convictions 97
courts 116
cross-disciplinary disputes 48
cynicism 79

D

deliberative democracy 79
deliberative mechanisms 75
deliberative rules 28
democracy 82
democratic decay and failure 29
democratic institutions 80
Derridean hierarchical opposition 62
deviant exit 48
diagnostic utility 99
disagreement
moral disagreement 5
ontological disagreement 2
semantic disagreement 2

disclosure of one's ontological position 113
disconfirmation conditions 101
disenfranchisement schemes 88
disputes, moral and political 17
disputes over Contestables: explanation, reduction, emergence, sufficiency 50
divergence patterns 104
divergent educational ontologies 87
dual-process theory (Greene) 4
due process 28
dyadic model of moral cognition (Gray) 4

E

effectiveness horizon
  appeals to clearer definitions fail 80
  body-cameras (policing) 62
  Contestables 24
  institutional stabilisation 18
  institution stabilisation 66
  sementic repair 5
Enlightenment ideals: reason, rationality, and logic 76
Enlightenment inheritance 109
Enlightenment promise 115–116
epistemic accounts 92
epistemic authority 61
epistemic deficit 101
epistemic disagreement 2
epistemic privilege 61
escalation by communication 75
escalation under dialogue 17
essentially contested concepts (Gallie) 21
evaluative terms: justice, threat, reasonable force, legitimacy, harm 42
evidence-based policies 54
evidential deficit 49
evidentiary standards 28
exit options 87
extremism 75
  extremism and failure 29

F

factual convergence 91
failure modes 89
federalism 86
federal sentencing guidelines 87

Feyerabend, Paul
hostile reception 50, 52, 112
exposing stabilisation mechanisms 56
methodological pluralism 52
Fluids 17, 102
formalisation of structural constraint model 33
formal vocabulary
structural constraint model 35
frameworks
frameworks (in science) 49
liberal frameworks 29
functionalism 49

G

genealogical shaping 8
graduate training 47
grant funding (as homogeneity gate) 48
Gray, Kurt
dyadic modal 4
moral judgment 3
premature conclusion 4
Greene, Joshua
dual-process theory 4
moral judgment 3

H

Habermas, Jürgen 73, 75–77
convergence by communication 75
Habermas' wager 75
Haidt, Jonathan
Moral Foundations Theory 4
moral judgment 3
heritability 56–57
heritability and IQ scores 51
heterodox environments 48
high-salience legal cases 97
hiring (as homogeneity gate) 48
hostile reception of Kuhn, Feyerabend, and Latour 56

I

improved deliberation (insufficiency of) 37
inclusion 88
Ineffables 22
institutional choice 87
institutional constraint 57, 98
institutional defensiveness (in science) 46
institutional ecology 47
institutional failure (misdiagnosis) 29
institutional filtering 48
privileged institutional mechanisms (in policing) 59
institutional ontology 61
institutional outcomes (underdetermination) 39
institutional research 106
institutional resources (finite) 50
institutional selection 57
institutional singularity 27–35, 94
institutions as mechanisms 116
intelligence research 53–54
interdisciplinary work 54
interpretation
  framework-dependent interpretation 53
  underdetermined interpretation 63
intersectional frameworks 102
Invariants 22
  body cameras 62
IQ dispute 51
irrationality 75, 79
irrationality and failure 29
isomorphic table for science and policing claims 68–70

J

jurisdictional separation 86
jury adjudication 66–67
jury selection 36
justice 83

K

Kuhn, Thomas
  hostile reception 50, 52, 112
    cxposing stabilisation mechanisms 56
  paradigms and incommensurability 52

L

Lakoff, George
  moral judgment 3
  moral reasoning 4
language abstraction 16
language complexity 15
language effectiveness 15–16
Language Insufficiency Hypothesis (LIH) 15, 53, 76, 104
language, perceived effectiveness 16
Latour, Bruno
  actor-network framing 52
  hostile reception 50, 52, 112
    exposing stabilisation mechanisms in science 56
legal verdicts 91–93
legitimacy 88
lesion studies 49
liberal optimism, tragedy of 77
limits of language, structural, under ontological divergence 75–76
limits of ontological diagnosis 109–113
local stability (of science terms) 46
loss distribution 86

M

maintenance 85–90
  maintenance as policy option 65, 77, 79–82
  maintenance, definition 86
  maintenance design levers 86
material coupling (in science) 45, 48–49
material coupling, ontological variance 57
measurement routines (in science) 48
medicine 53–54
methodological fit 48
methodology 101–108
misinformation 79
  misinformation and failure 29
modal loading 23
modernist inheritance 79
modern political theory 115
moral accusation 116
moral architecture, plural (legal) 99
moral authority, federalism (maintenance) 86–87
moral baseline 94
moral blueprints for harmony (Rawls, Habermas), why they fail 77

moral closure (legal) 97
moral cognition, affective and deliberative 4
moral cognition, architecture of 4
moral collisions, continment (maintenance) 86
moral community 23
moral conflict 1, 2, 5, 48, 80, 105
moral consequences 51
moral constitution (legal context) 92
moral containment (power) 117
contestable moral terrain, policing and adjudication 68
moral convergence (maintenance) 86
moral convergence through talk 117
moral danger (for institutions) 24
moral defect, asymmetric incomprehension 17
moral desert 74
moral disagreement 5, 8, 13, 33, 76, 79, 88, 115
  body-cams (moral disagreement) 62
  moral disagreement (maintenance) 85, 96
  persistent moral disagreement 73, 101
moral discourse 48
moral dispute 17, 55
moral domain (expectations) 56
moral domains, salience 102
moral equivalence (science and policing)(table entry) 68–69
moral evaluation 3, 63
  moral evaluation (legal) 93
moral exhortation (quietism) 111
moral facts 13, 111
moral failing 77
moral failing, not (scientists) 54
Moral Foundations Theory (Haidt) 4
moral ideal (maintenance) 81
moral imagination (legal verdicts) 91
moral, incompatible conclusions (legal) 97
moral indictment (power) 39
moral indictment (science) 52
moral injury (legal) 97
moral institutions 4, 46
moral intolerance (science) 59
moral judgment 3–4, 13, 104
  ontological indexing 110
  policing and jury adjudication 66
moral jurisdiction (table entry) 11
moral language 104

moral legitimacy (maintenance) 87
moral loading 57
moral loss (maintenance) 87
moral narratives (diagnostic) 103
moral objectivity 4
moral opacity 75
moral orientations, Lakoff 4
moral outrage, failure mode (table entry) 70
moral persuasion 40
moral persuassion strategies 115
moral plurality 86
moral preferences 9
moral properties 13
moral psychology 3, 9
moral public, failure 116
moral reaction 65
moral realism 13
  moral realism as an ontological vector 111
  moral realism, scepticism toward 109
moral reasoning, Lakoff 4
moral reconciliation 88
moral relativism (why not) 110
moral risk 56
moral salience 12
  moral salience as ontological vector 111
  salience of harm 75
moral seriousness (Galllie) 24
moral sophistication 68
moral standing 23
moral status 51
moral stubbornness 15
moral, temporal scope (table entry) 11
moral terms (nomenclature) 37
moral theory 115
  contemporary moral theory 17
moral tolerance 103
moral truth 13
moral truth, adjudication 112
moral types (table entry) 10–11
moral valence 65
  moral valence (legal) 98
moral victory 111
myth of resolution (in law) 96

N

naïve inference of politics in re science 45
narrative elicitation 104
nature-nurture dispute 51
neuroimaging data 49
nihilism, charge of 81
non-compliance as a potential escalation vector (in policing) 60
non-reductive accounts 49

O

objectivity (in science) 47
officer testimony (in policing) 61
ontological acculturation 47
ontological agreement (doesn't exist) 93
ontological assimilation 82
ontological asymmetry 61
ontological collision 2, 54
ontological conflict management 82
ontological convergence 39
ontological dimensions 93
ontological disagreement 2, 50
ontological disclosure 109–113
ontological divergence 51, 65, 88
ontological engineering 60
ontological evaluation 95
ontological fault-lines 12
  ontological fault-lines (table entry) 11
ontological fit 48
ontological homogeneity
  local ontological homogeneity 45, 61
  selection, training, and manufacture 46
ontological indexing 56
ontological mediation 55
ontological neutrality (no view from nowhere) 109
ontological orientation 1–2, 7–13, 47, 49, 74, 76, 102–103
  incompatible ontologies 51, 101
  instantiation of ontological orientation 67
  negation of ontological orientation 67
  ontological divergence 17, 28
  ontological orientation (in policing) 67
  plural ontological orientations 21
  table entry 27

ontological plurality 12, 23, 29, 34, 37, 40, 85
dynamics of ontological plurality 56
illusory ontological plurality 55
managing general dynamics of ontological plurality 46
recognition of ontological plurality 88
ontological selection 42
ontological selection under time pressure (in policing) 67
ontological variance 51
ontological variance reduction (in policing) 59
ontology
institutional ontology 61
plural ontologies, discource non-convergence 75
orientation
asymmetric ontological orientation 24
incompatible ontological orientation 22
plural ontological orientations 24
outcome selection 94
outcome stabilisation, through authority 59
outrage 64
asymmetric outrage 2, 5, 29, 67, 68, 97
dissolving outrage (police reform) 64
invariant outrage with respect to outcome 95
moral outrage, mistaken for bad faith 70
outrage invariance 91
performative outrage 37
persistent outrage 29, 81, 91
predictable patterns of outrage 64
procedural appeals, aggrevate outrage 96

P

paradigm discontinuities (in science) 46
paradigm shift 52–53
pathology as default diagnosis 79
USA PATRIOT Act 87
peer review (as homogeneity gate) 48
persistence after clarification 17
persistent controversies (of science terms) 46
persistent outrage 29
p-hacking 54
plea bargains 98
pluralism, collective decision-making under 4
plurality, irreducible 5

polarisation, affective 79
polarisation, failure to reduce 99
polarisation of highly-educated groups 76
police discretion 66–B-136
police reform 63
policing 59–75
political competence 88
Political Liberalism 74
power and Contestables 41
power and Invariants 41
power and the illusion of neutrality 42
power as a tool 117
power as functional mechanism 40
power as mediation 29, 39–41
power, endorsement of 79
power, exogenous 2
power-mediated settlement 56
power mediation 88
power, non-acquiescence 88
power, role of, explicit and implicit 96
power, semantic failure 41
power, three forms
  hard power: coercive settlement 40
  soft power: norm-setting & agenda control 41
  structural power: path dependence & institutional inertia 41
prediction and control 49
prestige mechanisms (as homogeneity gate) 48
presumption gap 16
pre-verbal orientations 5
procedural appeals (why they fail) 95
procedural legitimacy 95
procedural visibility 87
procedure 28–29
promotion (as homogeneity gate) 48
psychology 53–54
publication bias 54
punishment proportionality (in criminal sentencing) 74

Q

quietism 79
  (why not) 111

R

rational convergence 73–75
rationalist myth 46
Rawls, John 73–77, 79
  public reason 79
reasonable force (as Contestable) 96
reasonable pluralism 74
recruitment of police 60
reductive physicalism 49
reflexivity of ontological diagnosis 109–113
reform, police 63, 82
  why police reform cycles fail 96
relativism, moral (why not) 110
replication crisis 53–54
replication (in science) 47
research programme 101–108
resolution, institutional 53
rotation (as policy) 87

S

safeguards, procedural 28
salience, architecture (legal verdicts) 99
salience, assignment of 40, 49, 56, 67
salience, assignment of ontological orientation 1
salience, assignment of pre-verbal 75, 101
salience, assignment (upstream divergence) 96
salience, asymmetric (moral realism) 13
salience, dimentional structure (in-group v. out-group) 12
salience, evaluative moral judgment (downstream operation) 3
salience, evaluative, ontological fault-line (table entry) 11
salience, high-salience (indexing) 3
  salience, science v. policing (table entry) 68–69
salience, high-salience legal cases (asymmetric outrage) 97
salience intensification (under clarification) 75
salience, judgment 67
salience mapping 103
salience, moral 12
salience, moral disagreement (not merely epistemic or semantic) 5
salience, multidimentional ontological orientation 10
salience of harm, ontological fault-line (table entry) 11
salience, pattern of 10
salience, pre-verbal 80
salience, pre-verbal assignment 101

salience, pre-verbal (bridge to moral judgment) 104
salience, pre-verbal (Greene's dual-process account) 4
salience, pre-verbal operative structuring (ontological) 7
salience prior to reason 7
salience profiles 104
salience, shift in ontological orientations 102
salience structures (in policing – attention, risk, acceptable force) 60
salience structures (maintenance) 79
salience weighting, ontological orientation 9
scandals 54
school choice 87
scientific consensus 45
scientific controversies 53–54
scientific convergence 45–58, 48, 55
scientific convergence and politics 55
scientific disagreement 49
scientific method 46
scientific norms 51
scientific rhetoric 46
screening, background (in policing) 60
selection bias in scientific institutions 47
semantic confusion 101
semantic drfit, limits 48
semantic intervention 4
semantic reconciliation 39
semantic repair, failure 24
semantic substitution 104
settlement (legal) 98
shared data 56
shared empirical conditions 51
shared orientation and constraint 47
shared standards of evidence, explanation, legitimacy 46
shared technical language 50
singularity machines, institutions as 1, 28
singular outcomes, necessity of 28
standards of evidence, shared 46
structural constraint model 33–35
structural implication 98
structural invariance 99
structural isomorphism with policing and science 65
sunset clauses (as policy) 87
survivability 86
sustainability 81

T

temporal loading 23
term limits (as policy) 87
thick ethical concepts (Williams) 23
threat perception (in policing) 60
transparency requirements 28

V

variance damping 86
veil of ignorance (Rawls) 73–75
verdicts as maintenance 96
verdicts as second injury (in policing) 68

W

Williams, Bernard
  moral objectivity (fragility of) 4
world-relations, non-neutral distribution of (in science) 46

www.ingramcontent.com/pod-product-compliance
Lightning Source LLC
LaVergne TN
LVHW010838120826
845149LV00017B/3185

* 9 7 8 1 9 7 2 0 2 5 0 0 0 *